...carpe noctem

Matej Sack was born in Bratislava in 1985 and moved to Austria at the age of six. He studied Nutritional Sciences at the University of Vienna and is currently working on his PhD in Chemistry. His first book "Hard & Heavy - Graded Rock Guitar Solos" was published by Schell Music in 2011.

"Hard'n'Heavy - E-Guitar Sonatas" contains eight own compositions in note notation and tabs. The songs cover a variation of styles (in Metal) and are composed in standard tuning to be played clean, fingerpicked, distorted or hybrid-picked. The applied techniques include all the advanced ones like tapping, alternate picking, hybrid picking and sweeping. At this stage, capable of playing stuff like this, you're most likely a better skilled guitarist/composer than I am. However, I wanted to put together some ideas and write it down so I can share it with others for a justified price. Don't hesitate to leave comments whether you like it or not by sending me an email.

matej_sack@gmx.net

\m/ Black'n'Roll \m/

The author would like to thank Patrick Pazour for the correction of the manuscript and all kinds of other ideas and Susanne Pichler for making the cover.

Herstellung und Verlag:
BoD – Books on Demand, Norderstedt
ISBN 978-3-7357-8725-5

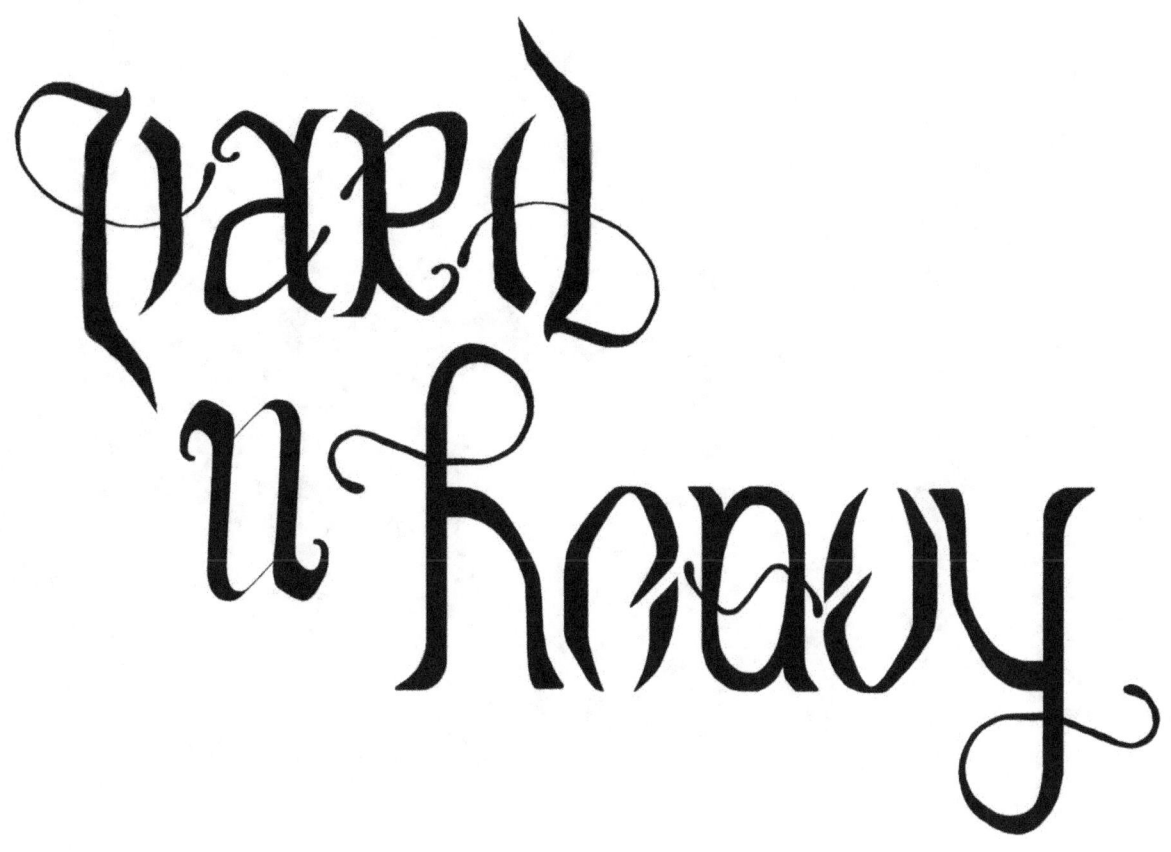

Matej Sack

terra insomnia	-1-
ferro ignique	-8-
only dust remains I&II	-13-
VII	-24-
legio solis	-27-
will-o'-the-wisp	-31-
nemoralis	-36-
caelestis	-40-

"Terra Insomnia"

Music by Matej Sack

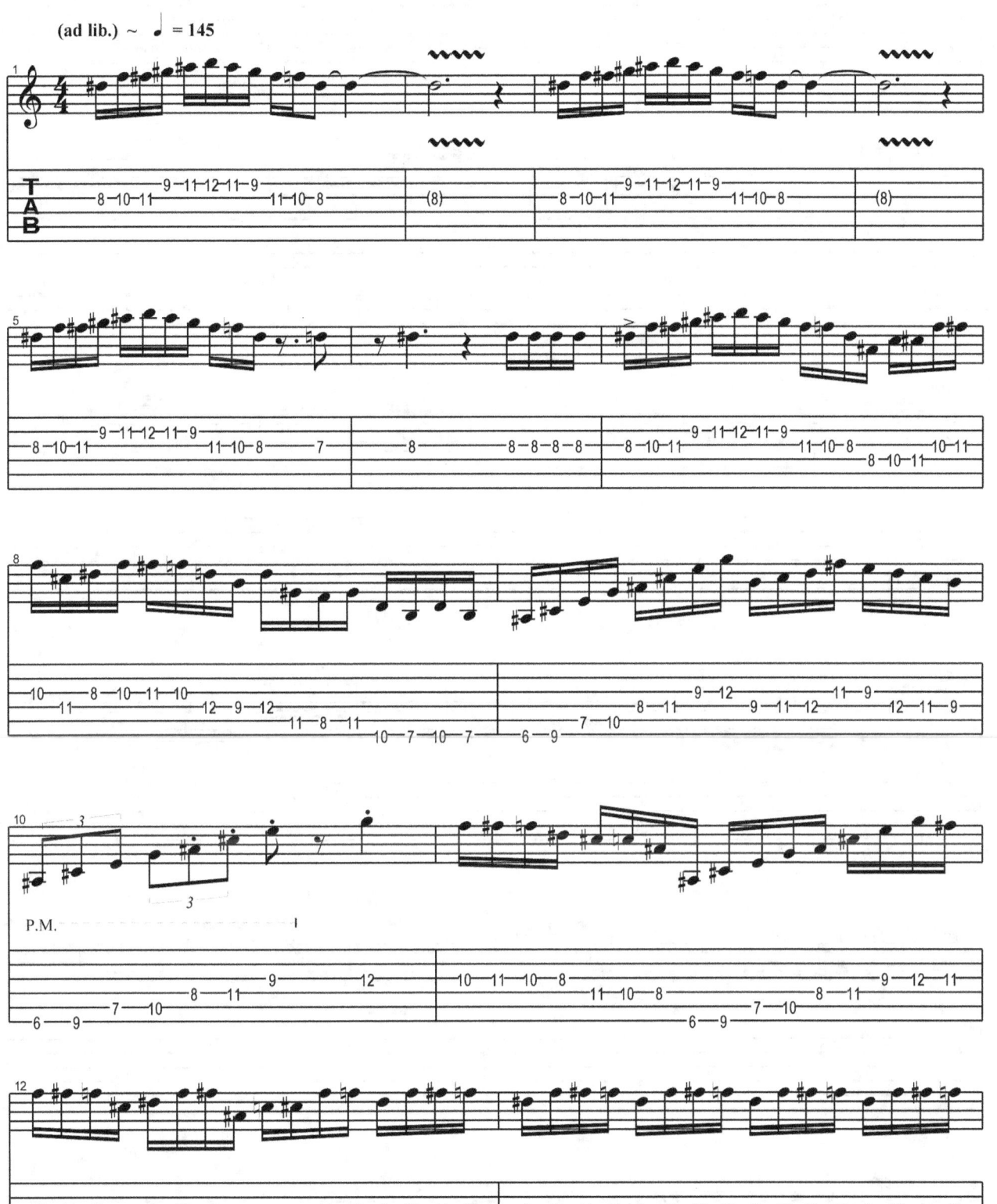

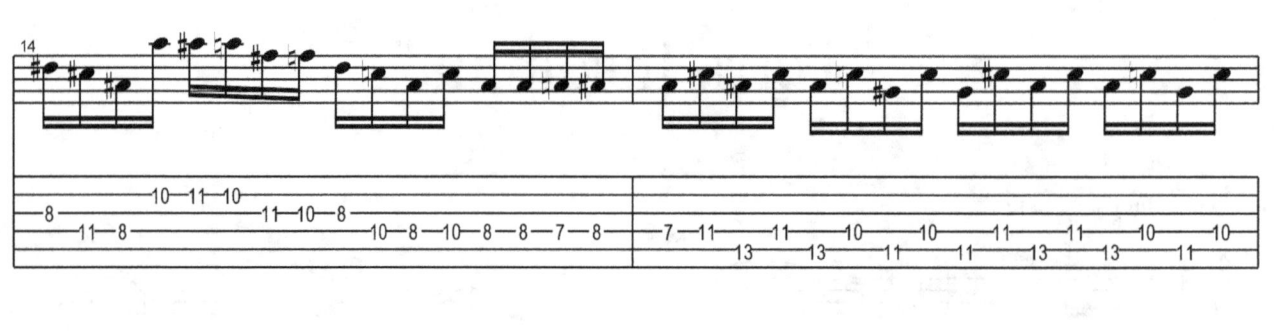
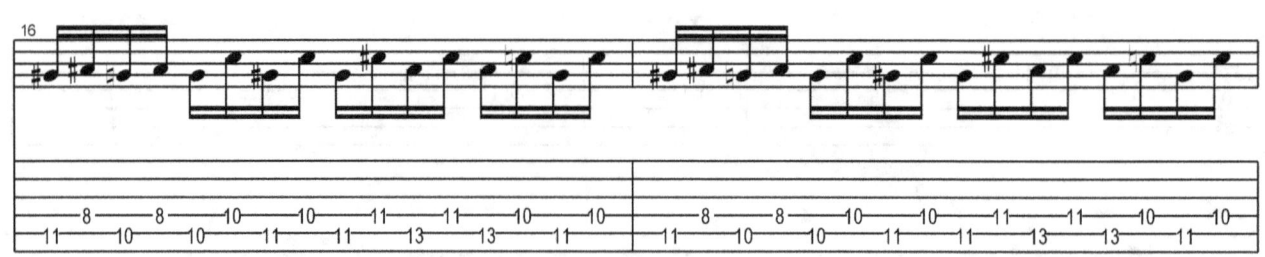
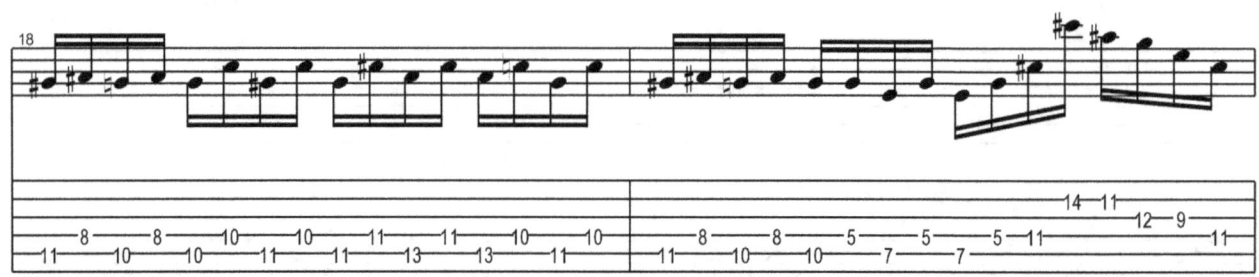
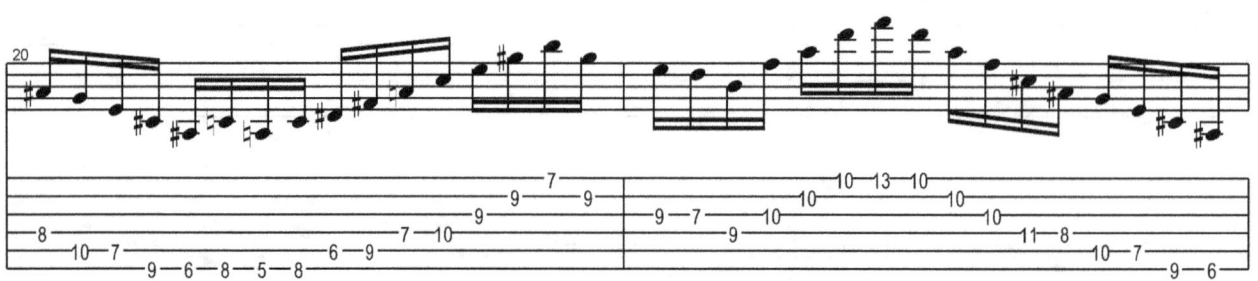
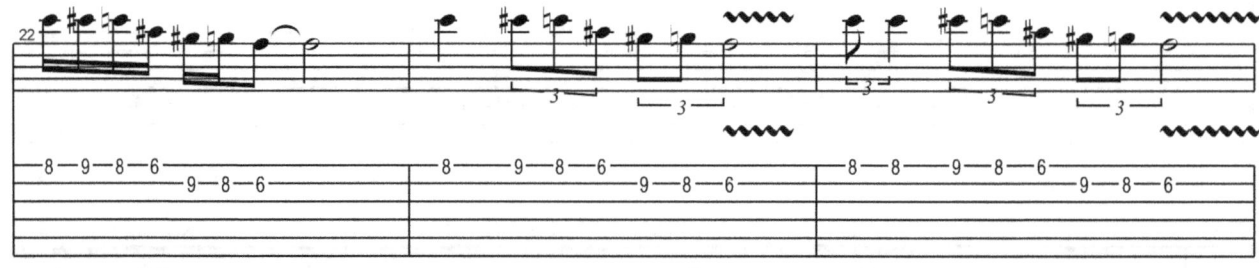
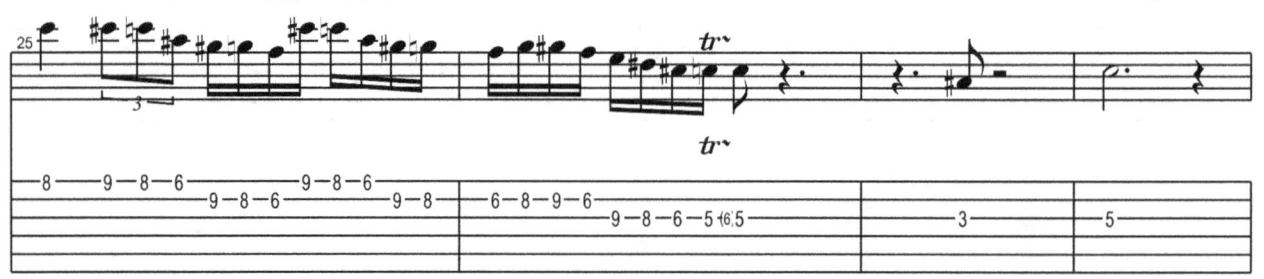

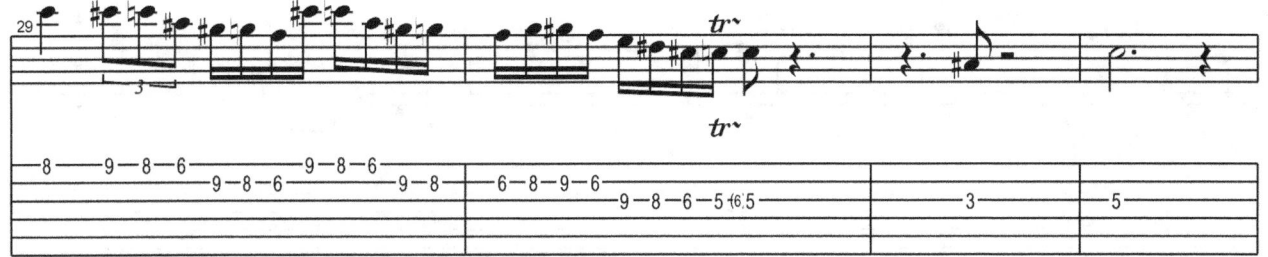
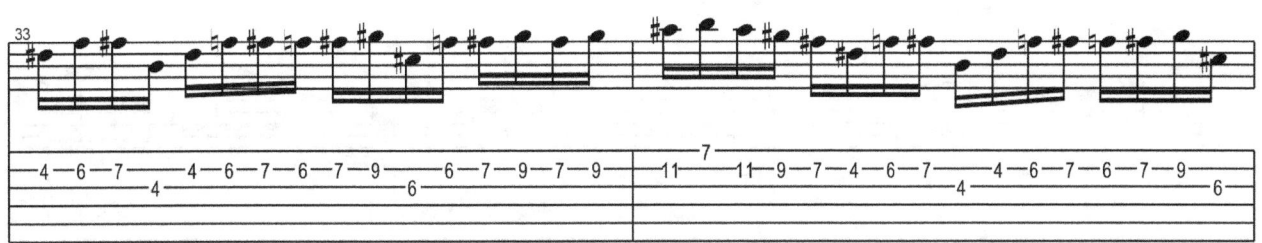
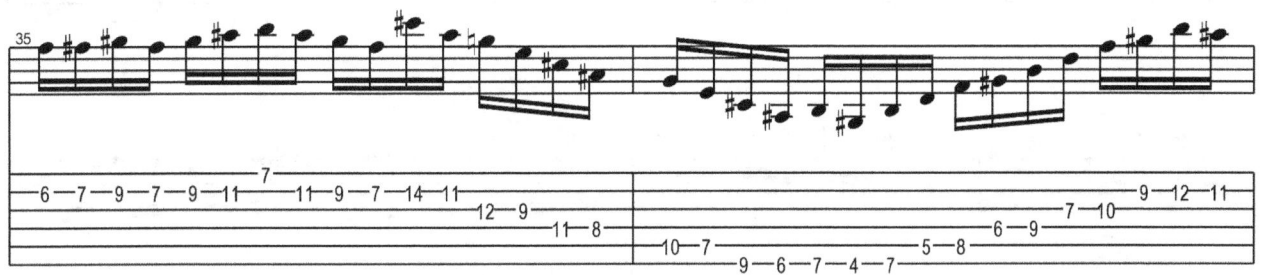
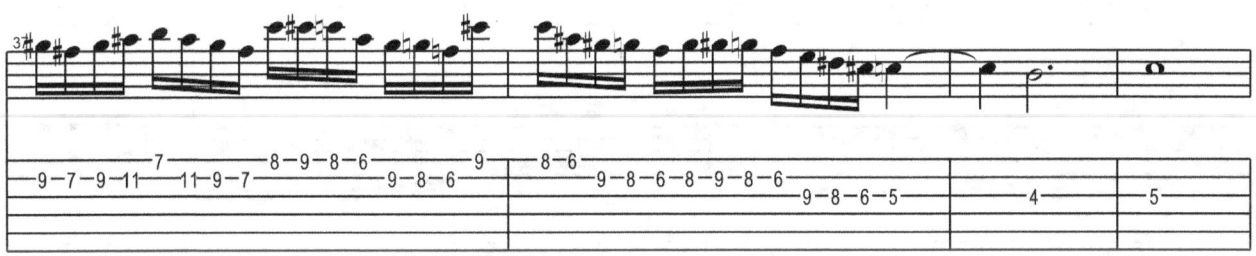
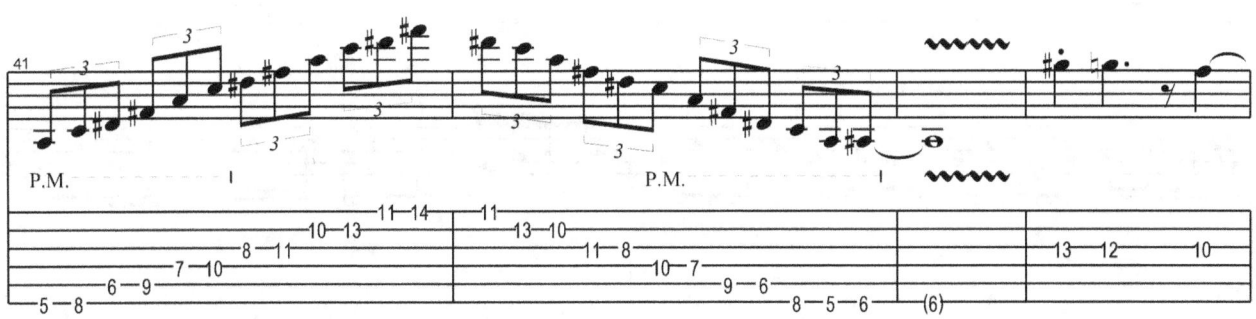
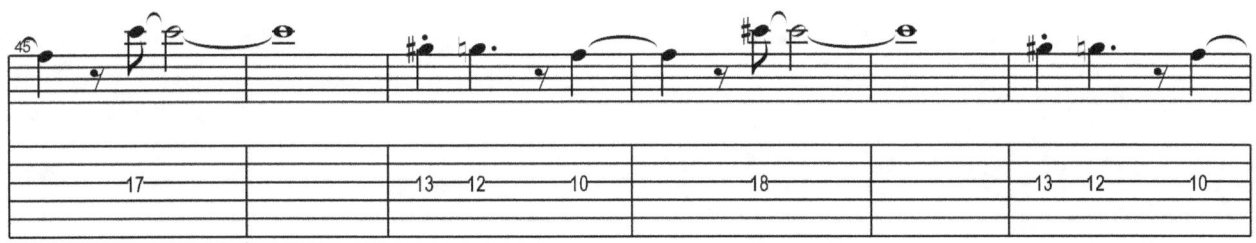

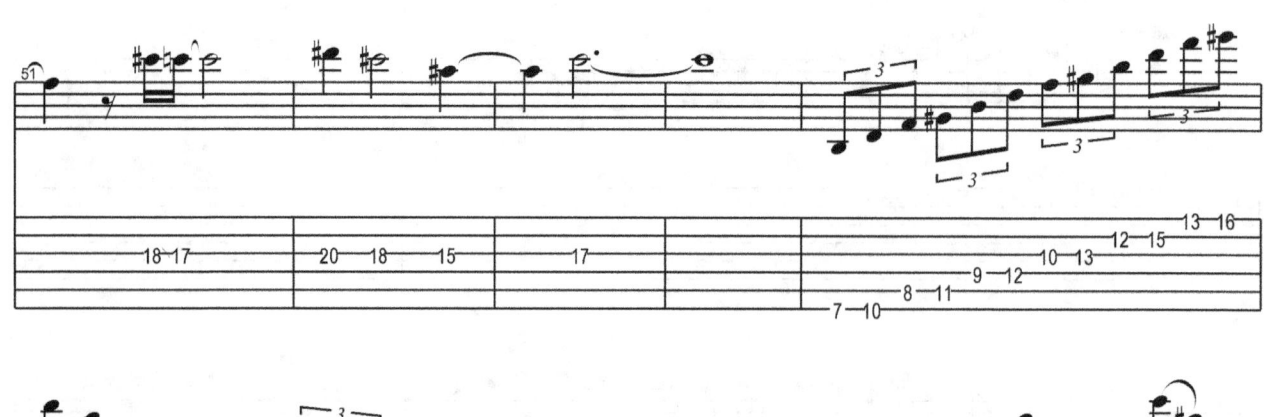
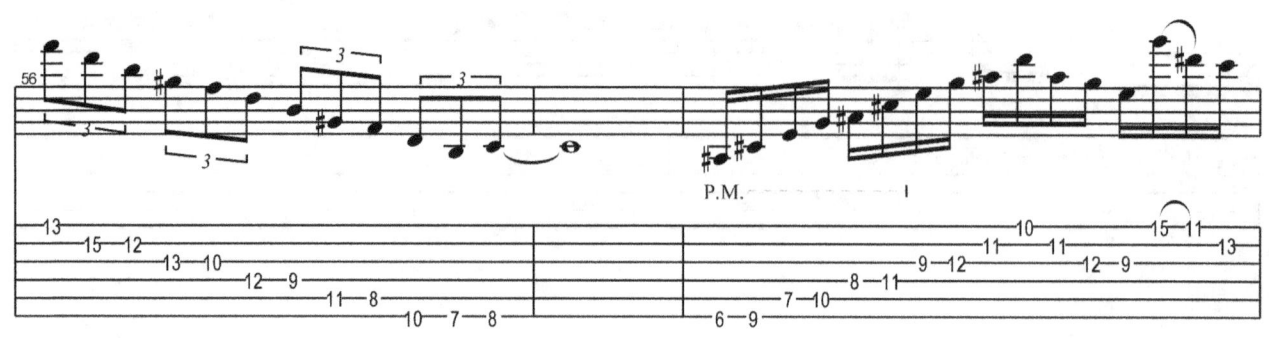
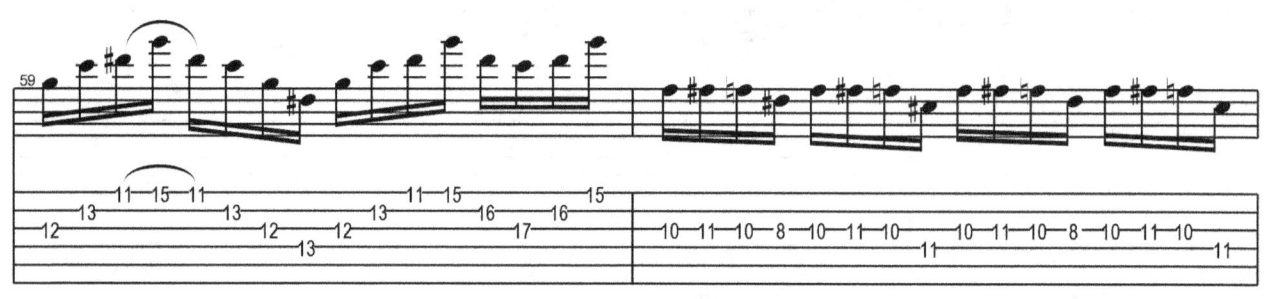
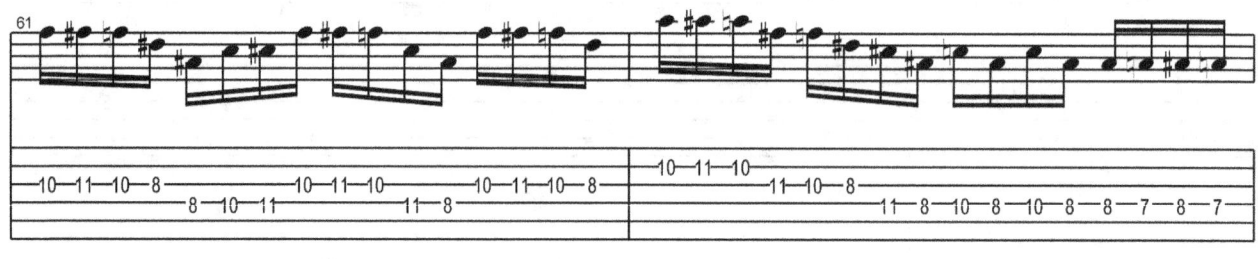
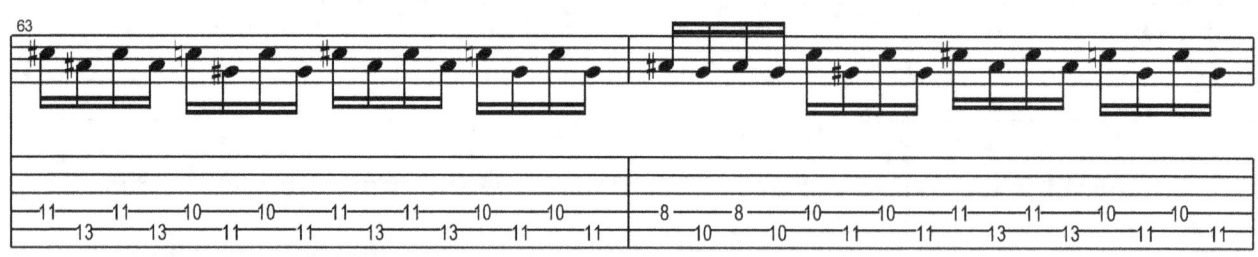

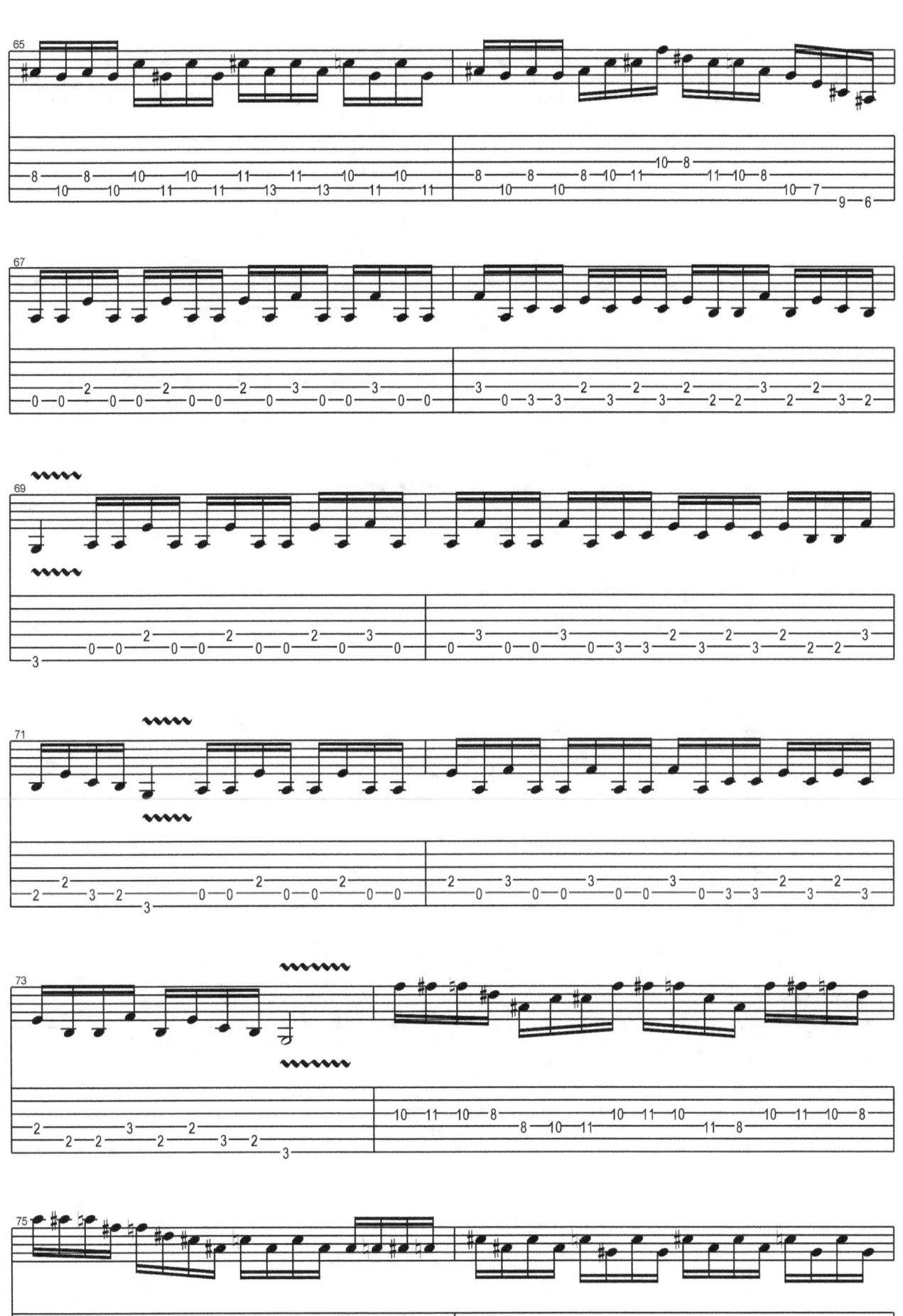

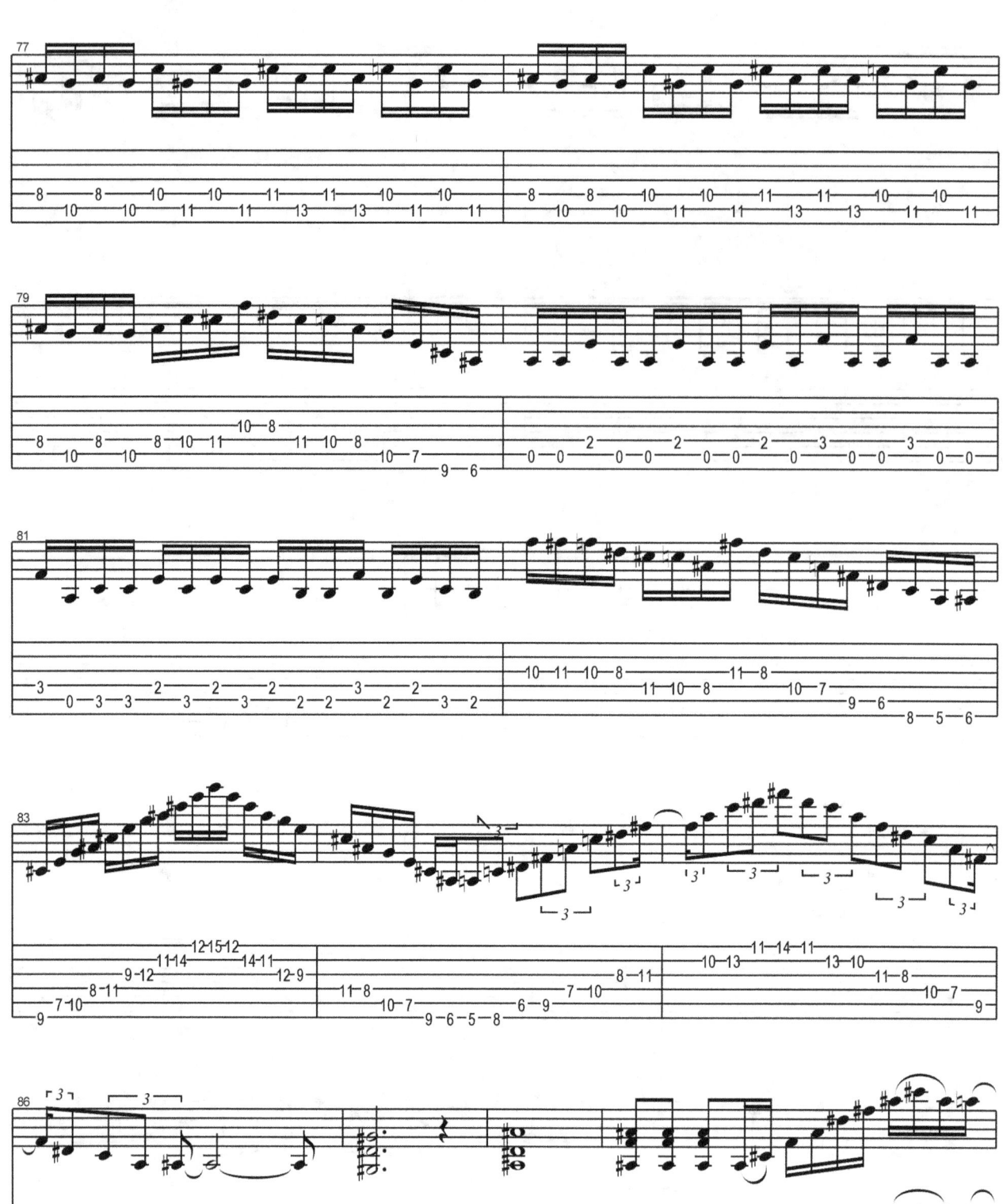

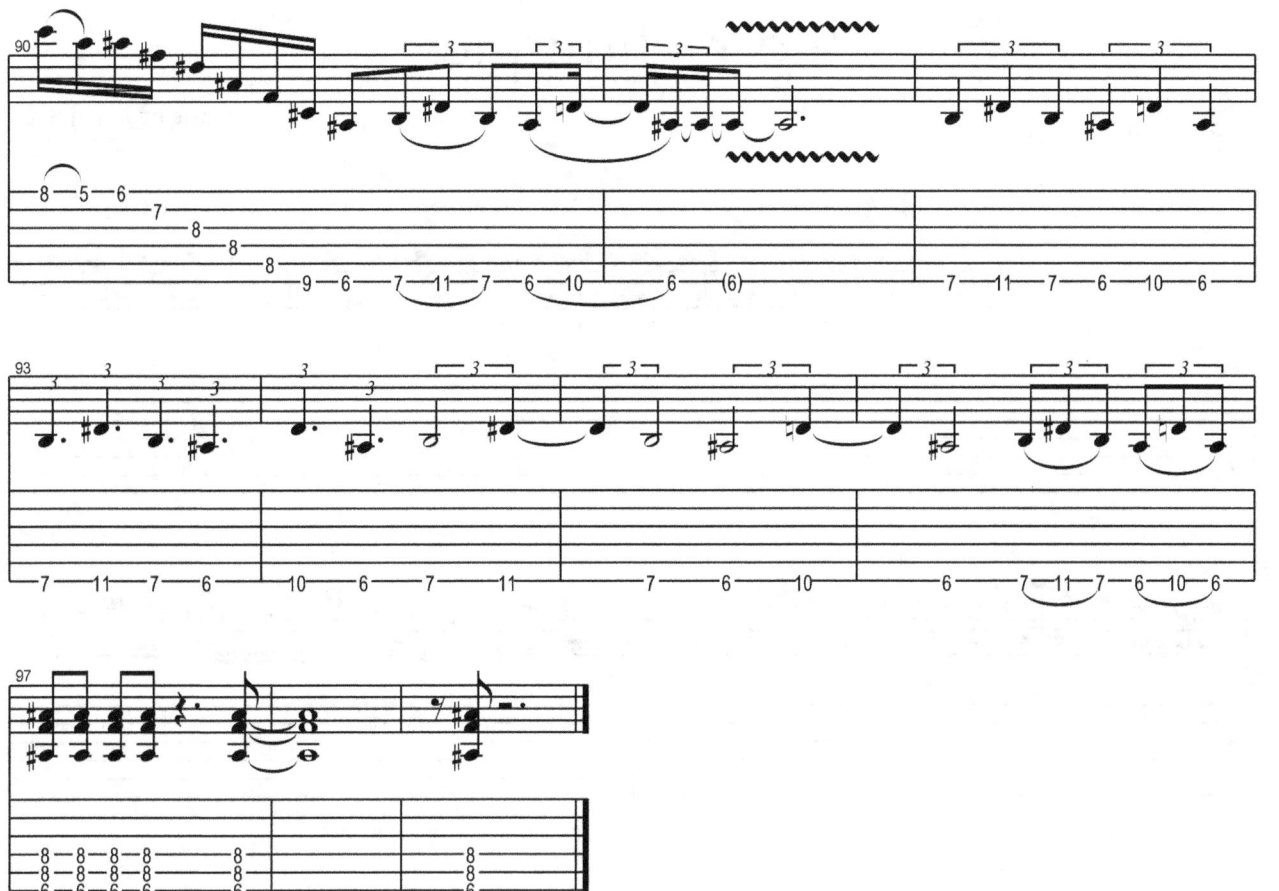

"Ferro Ignique"

Music by Matej Sack

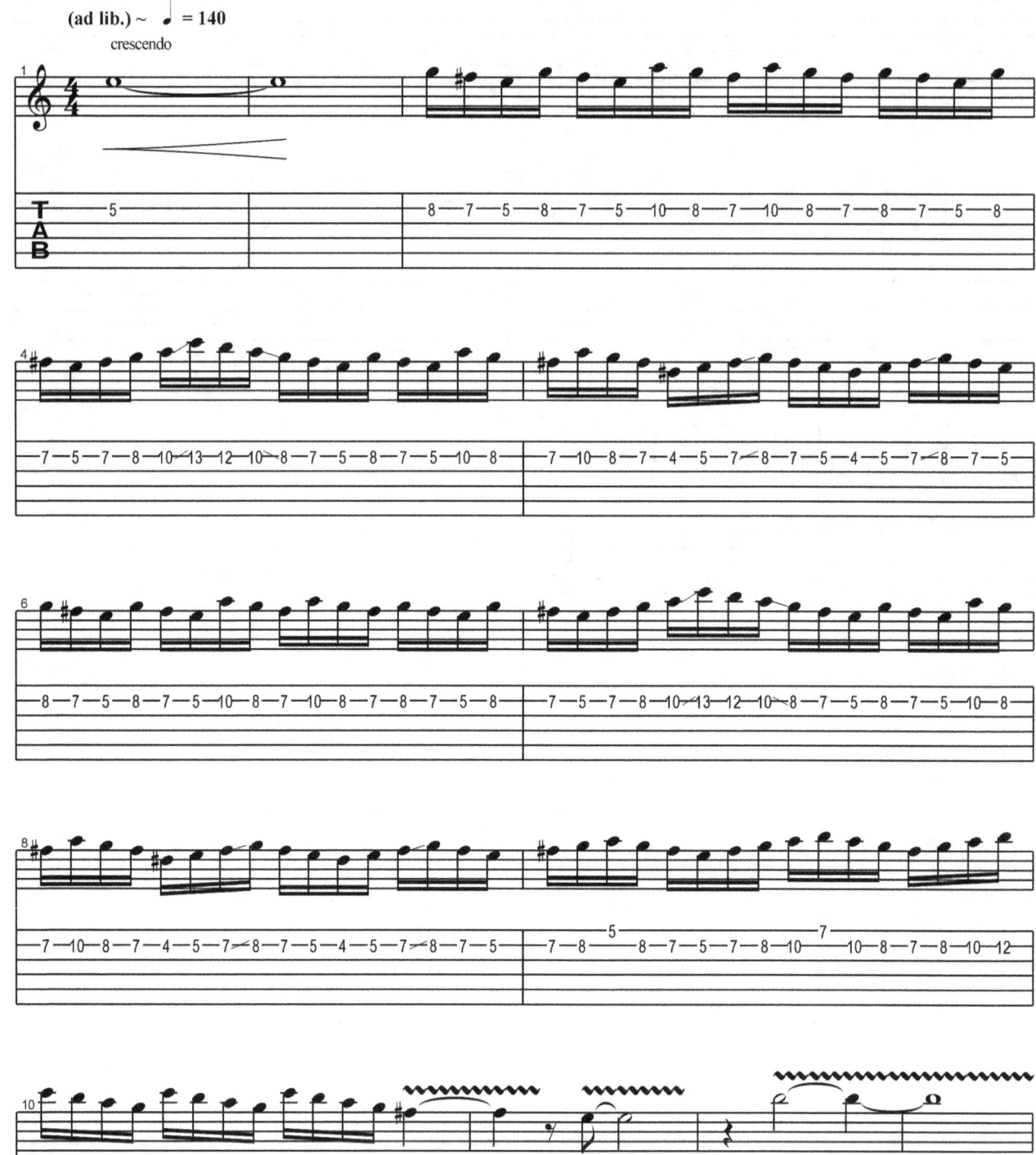

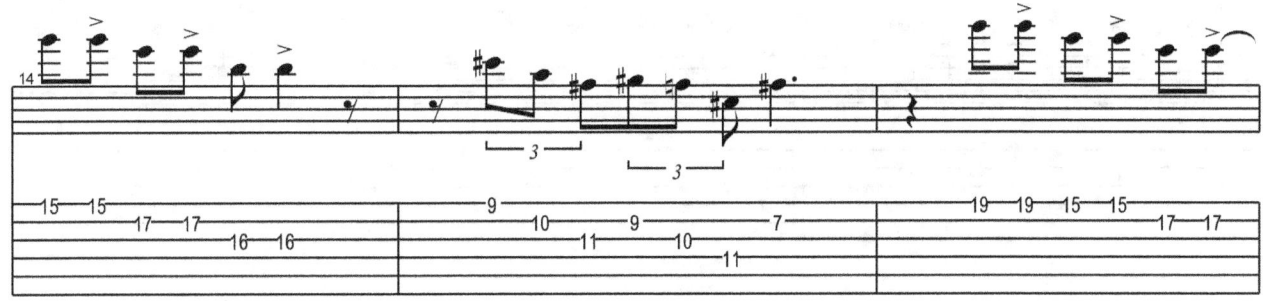
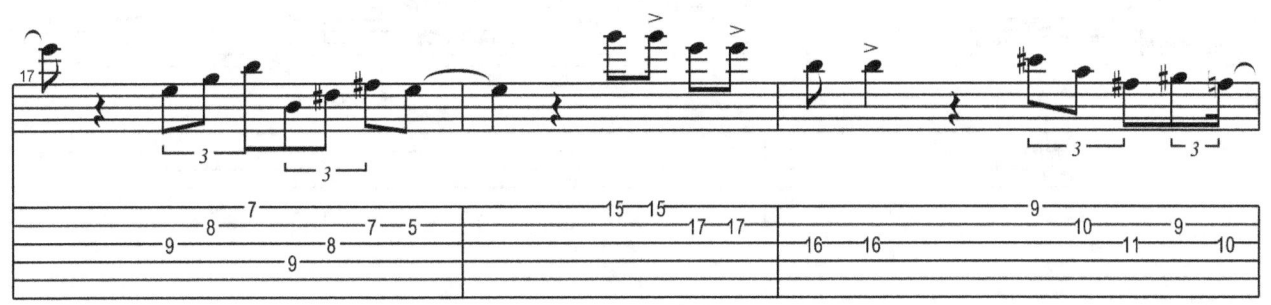
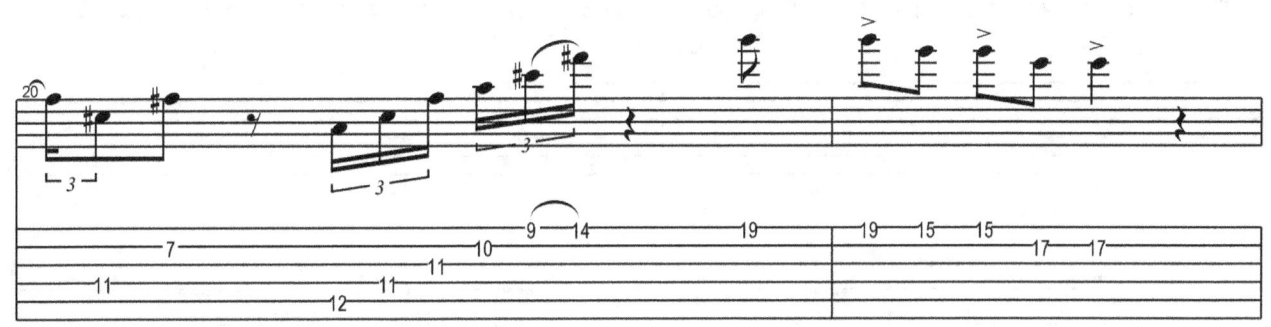
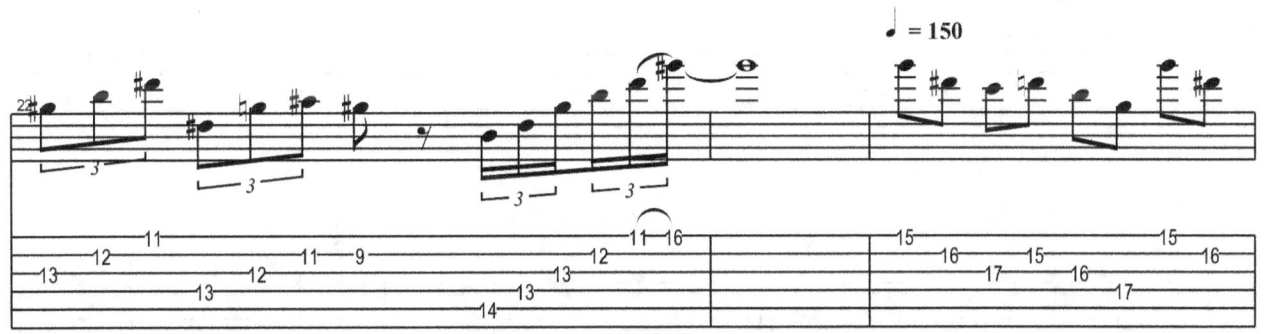
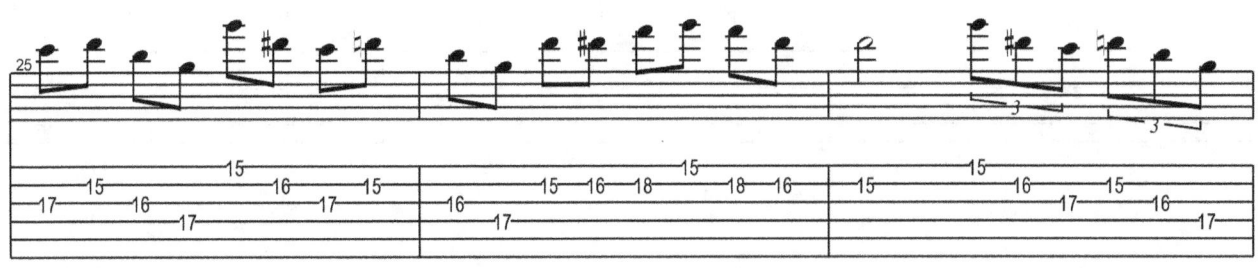

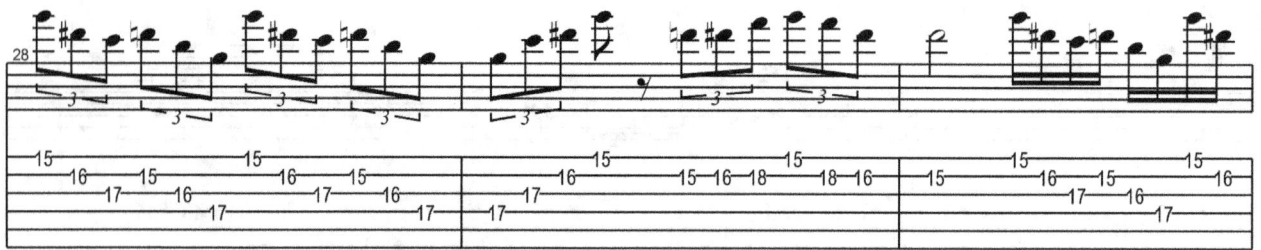
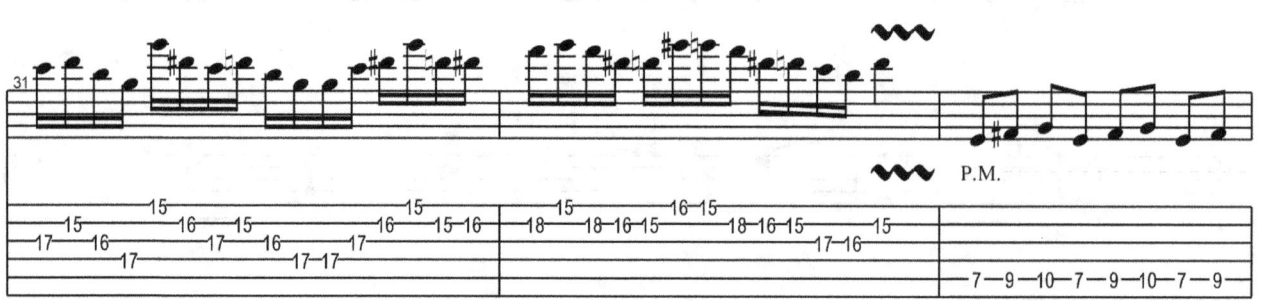
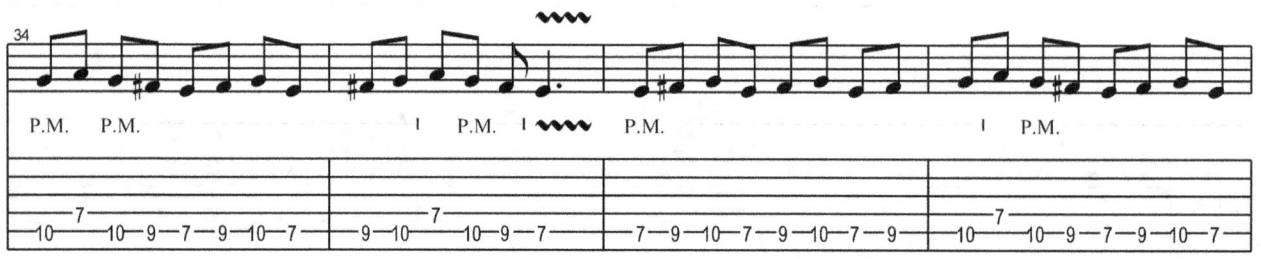
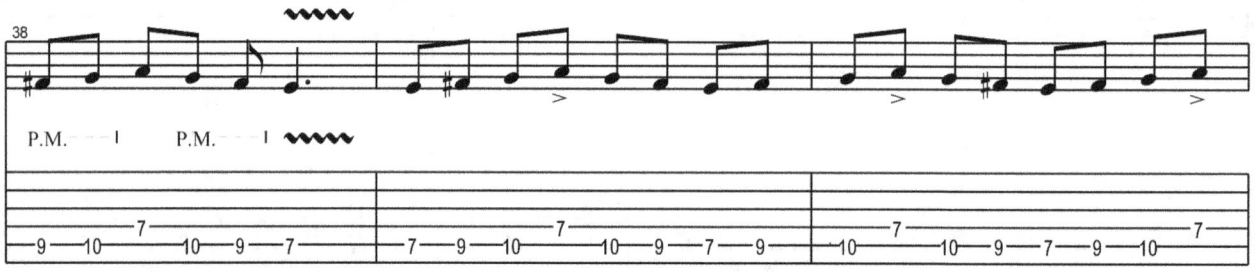
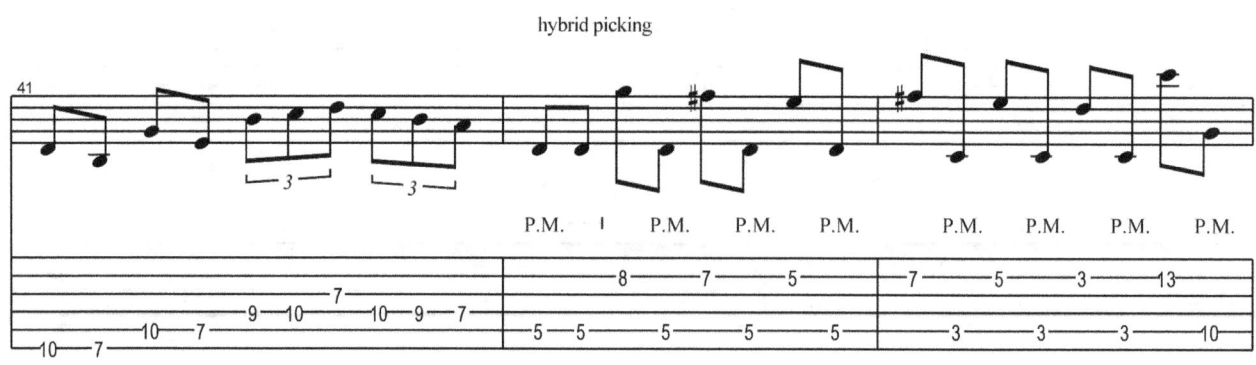

10

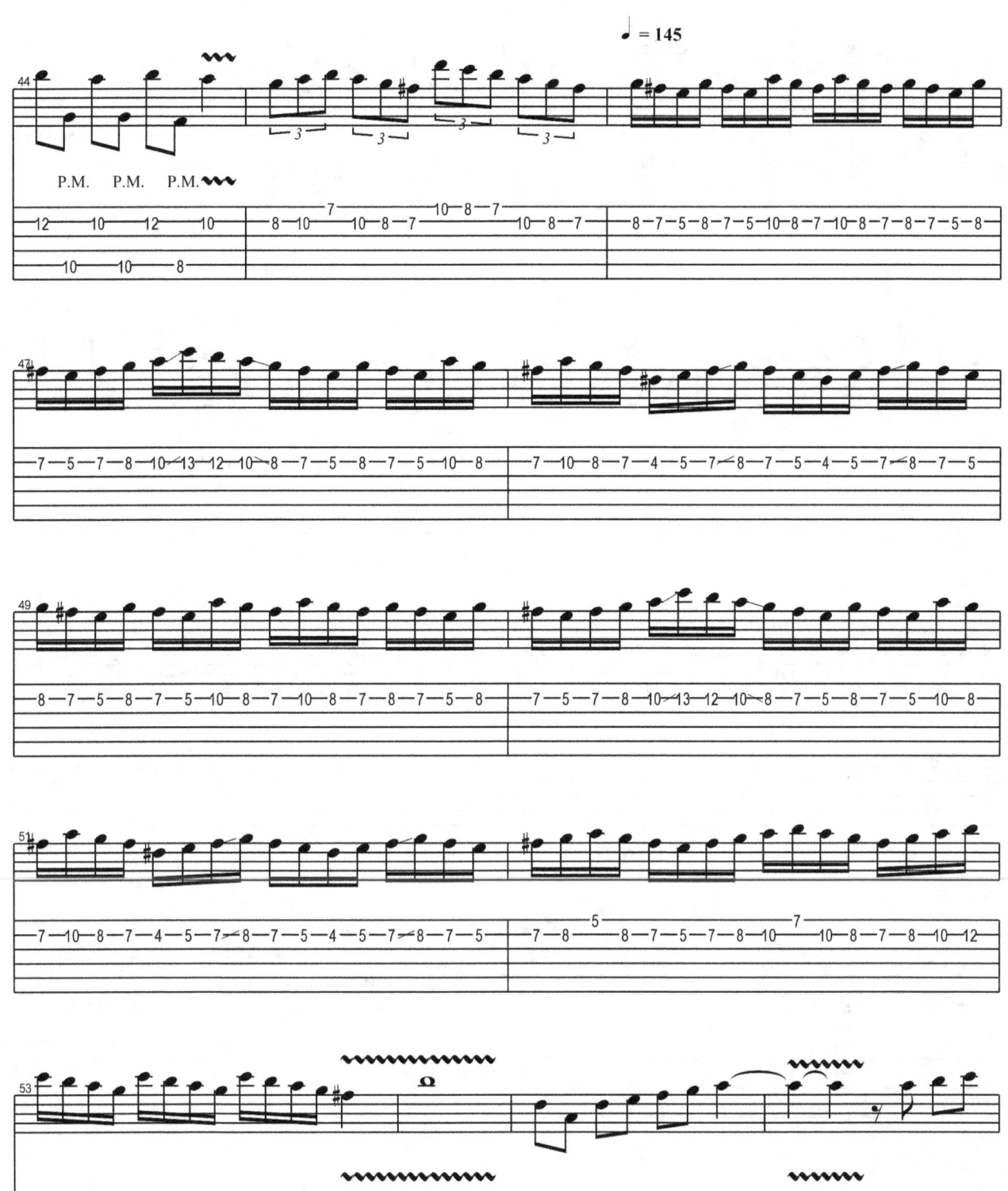

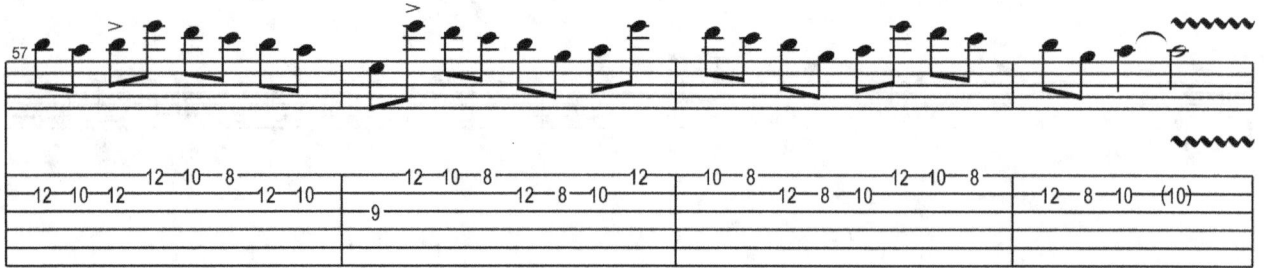
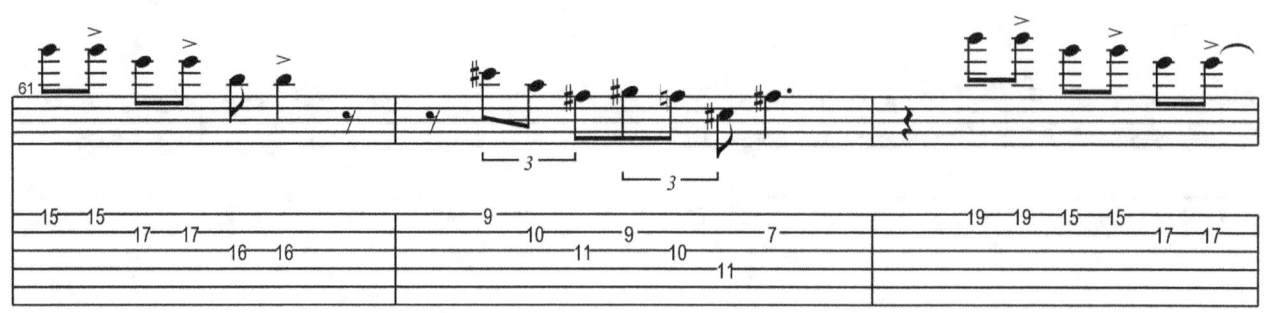
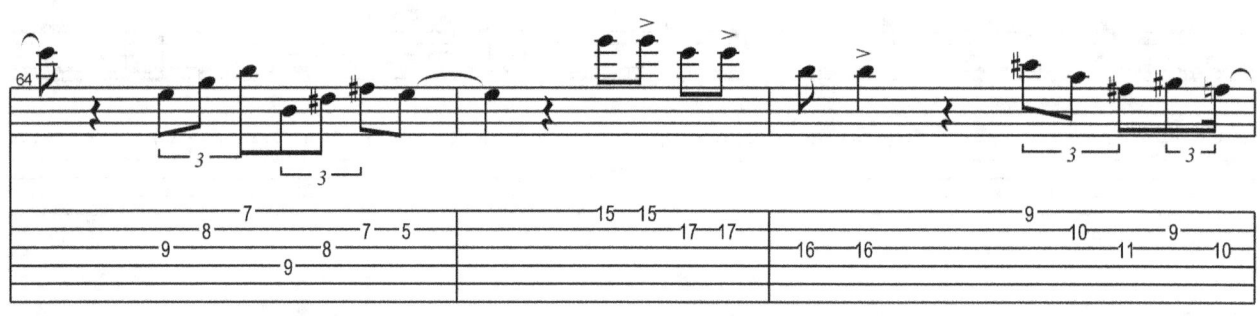
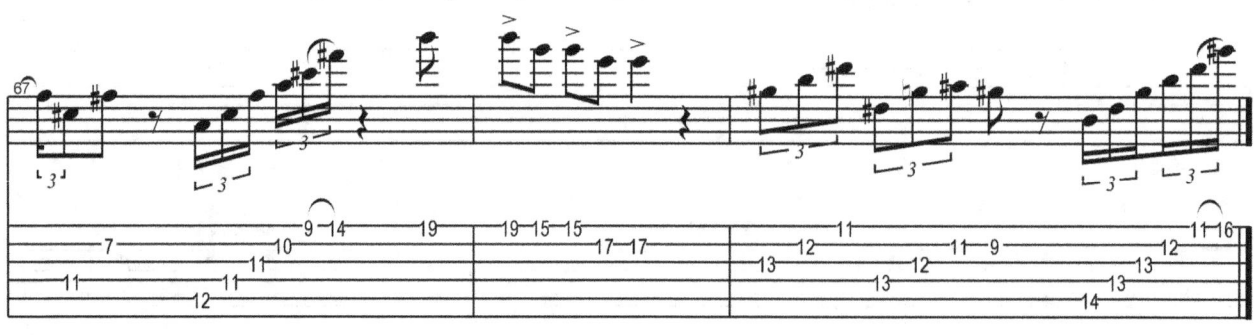

12

"Only Dust Remains"
Guitar 1

Music by Matej Sack

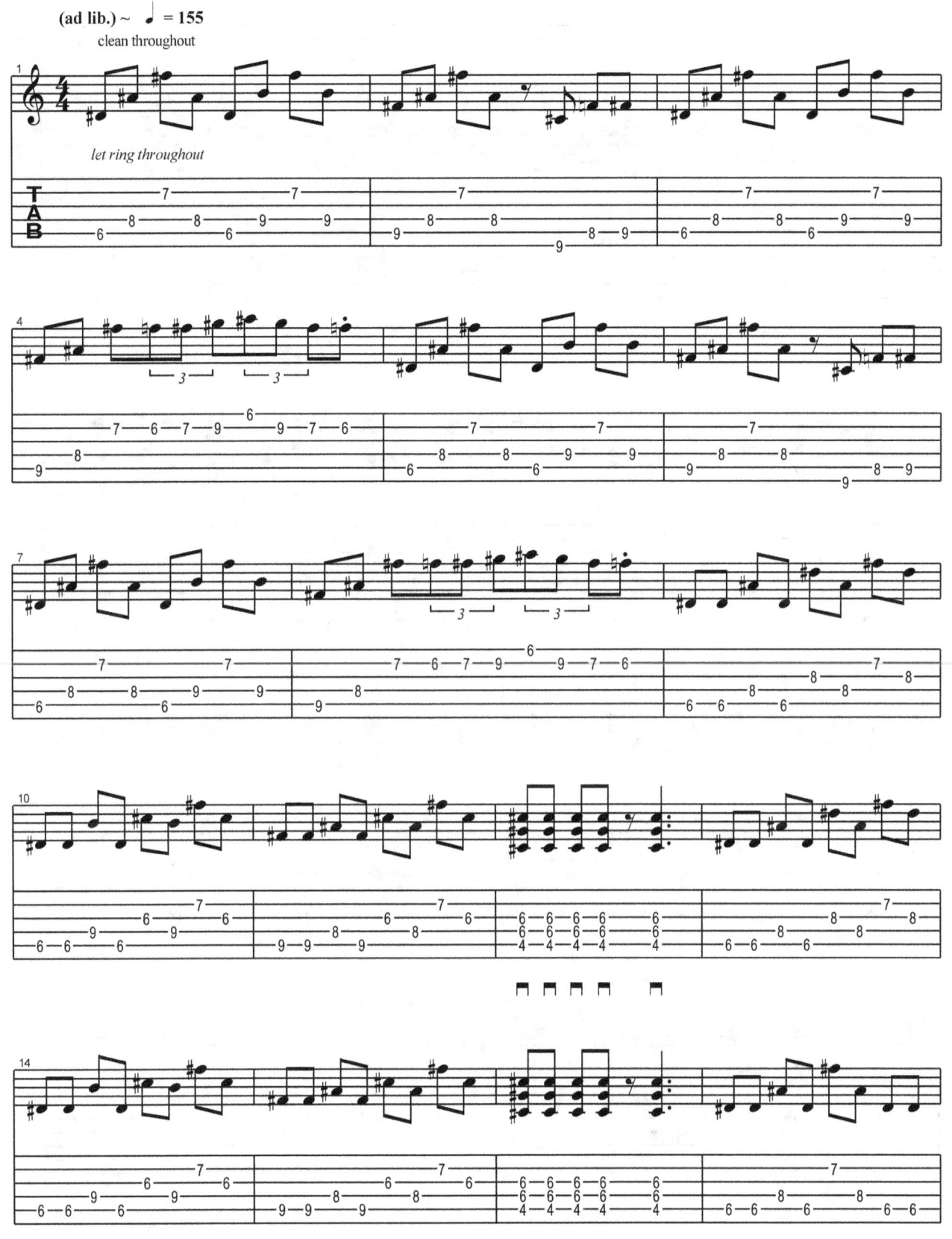

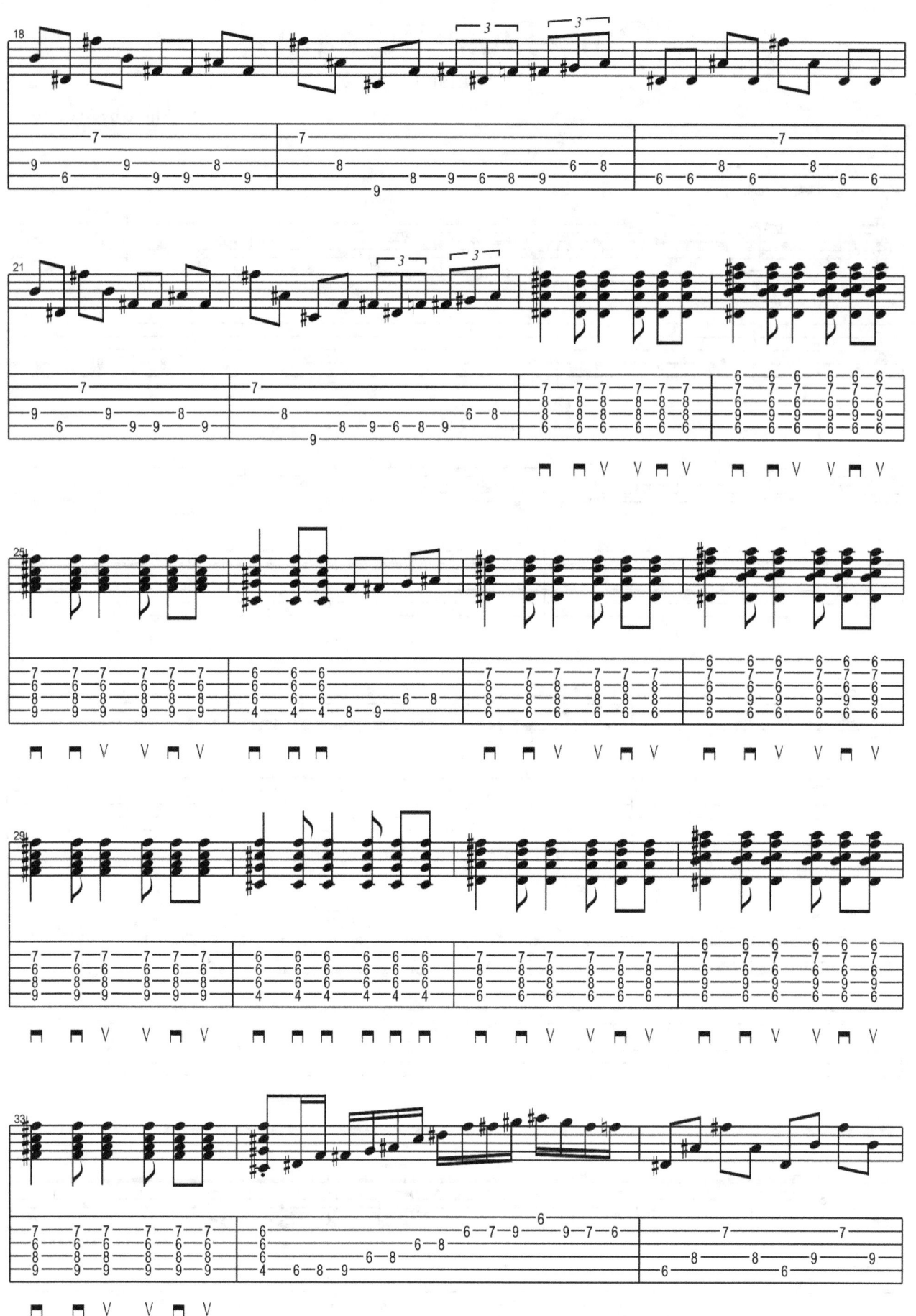

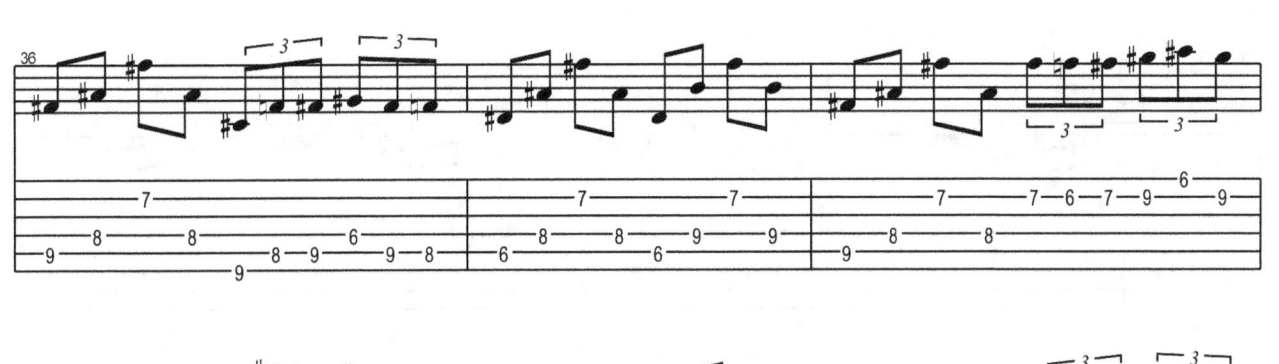
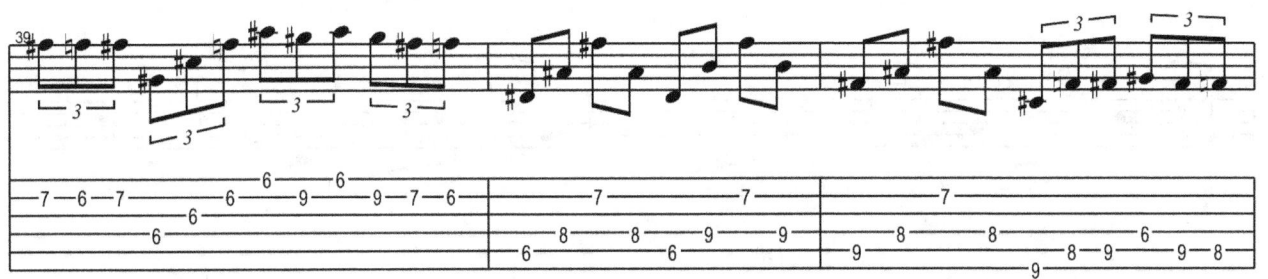
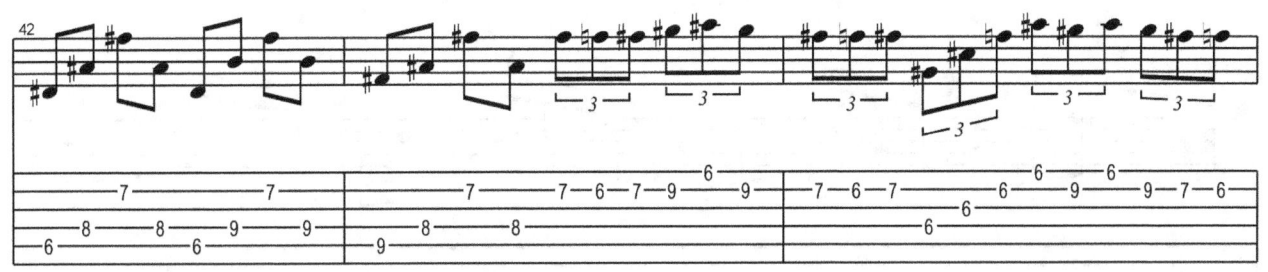
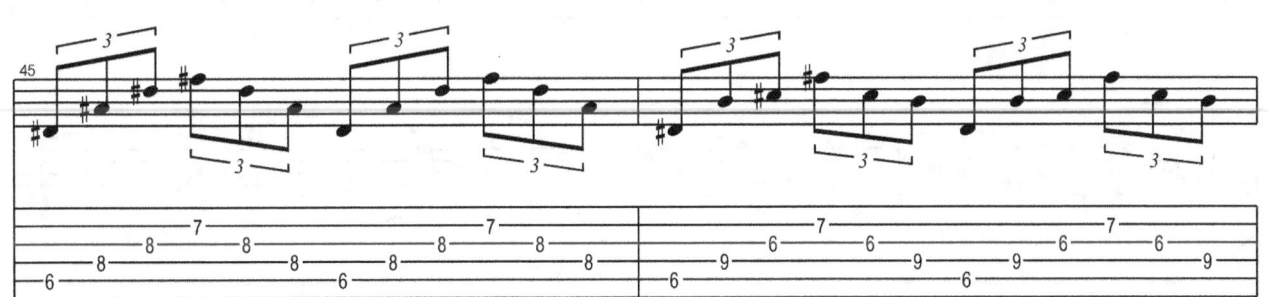
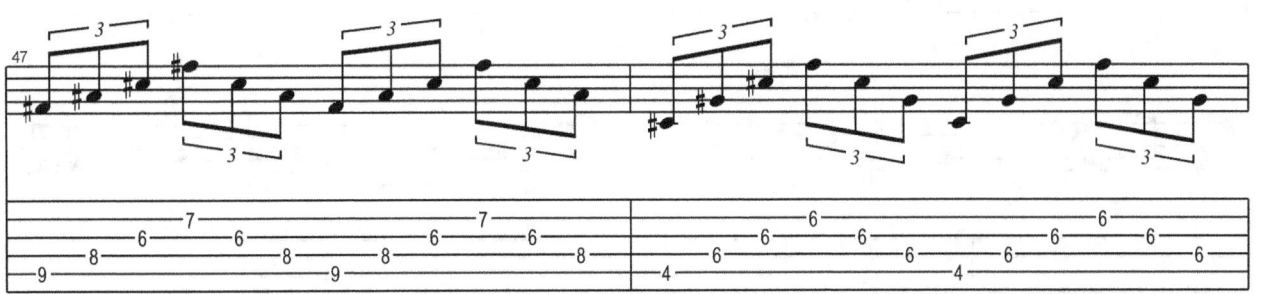

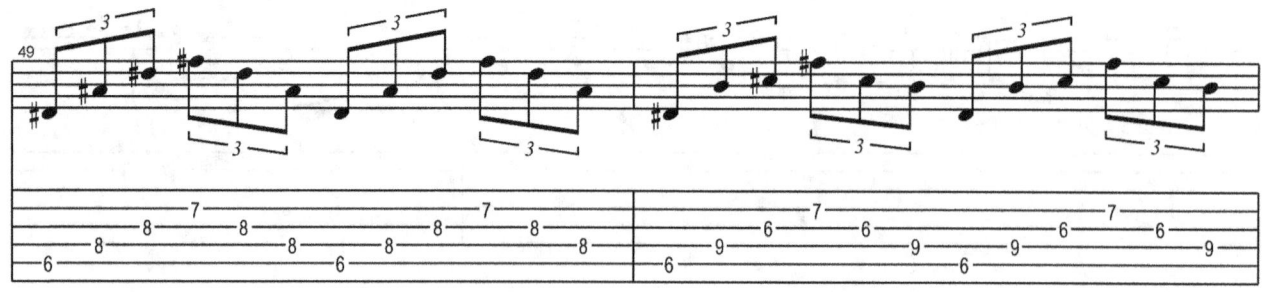
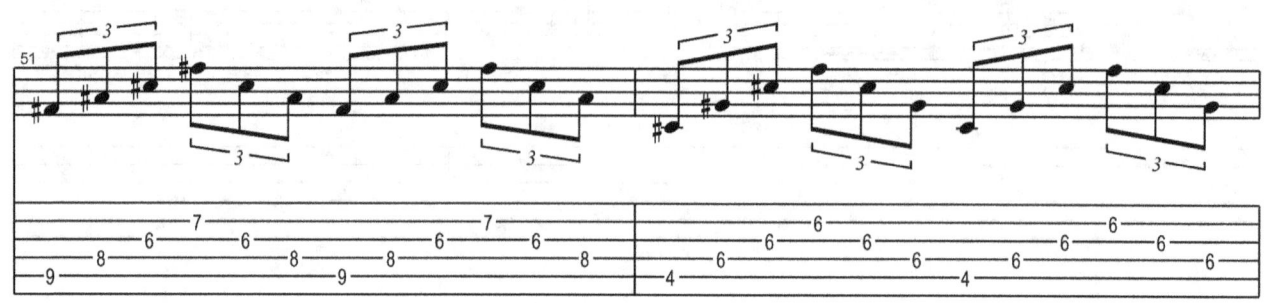
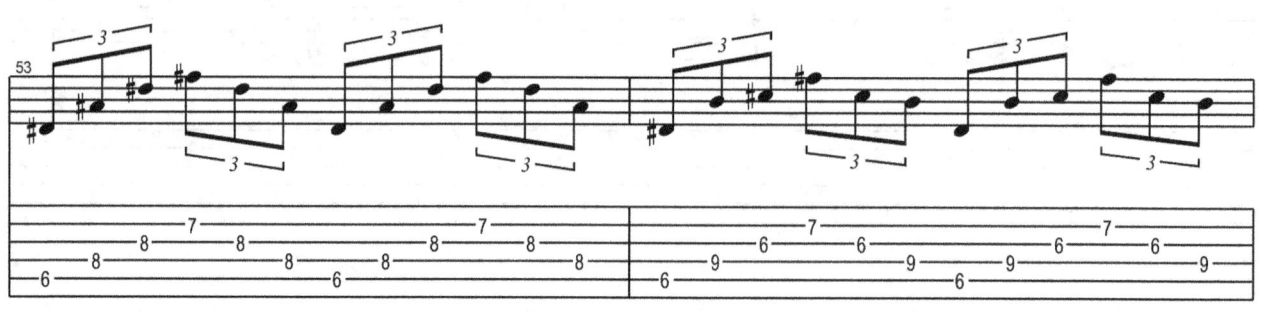
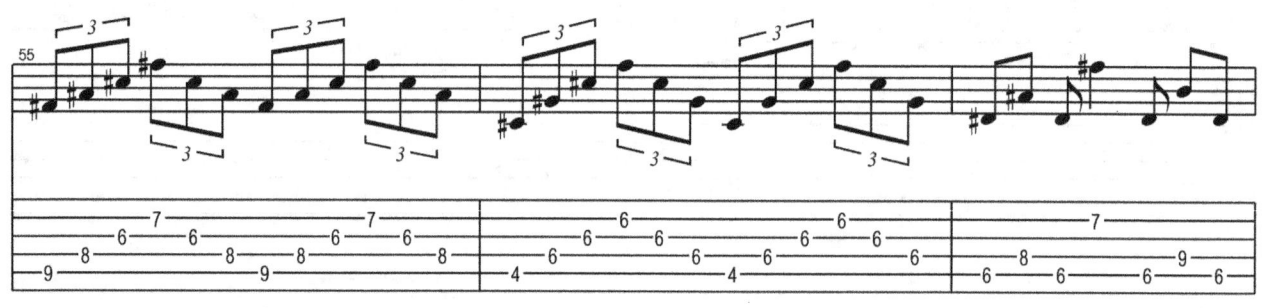
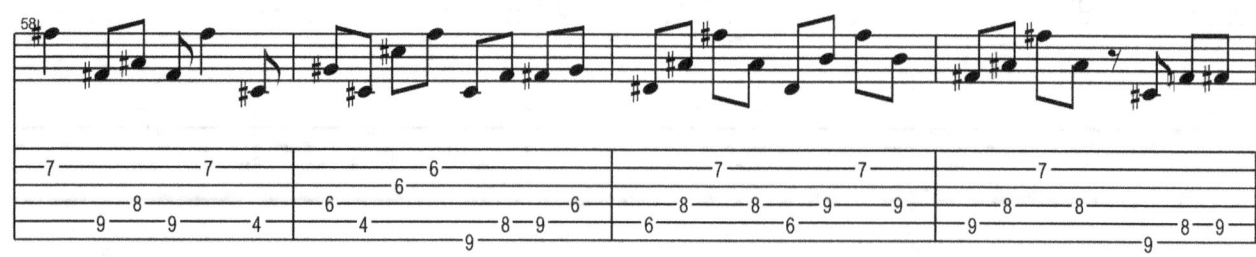

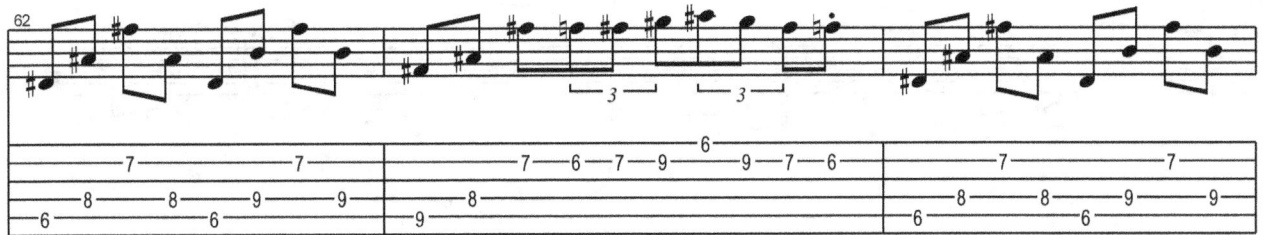
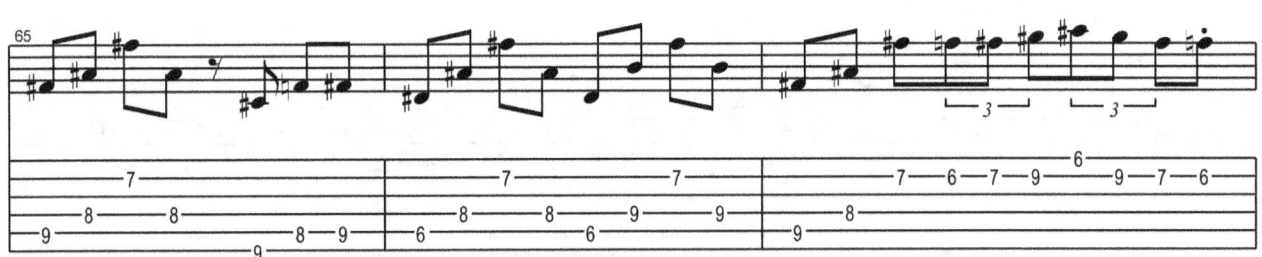
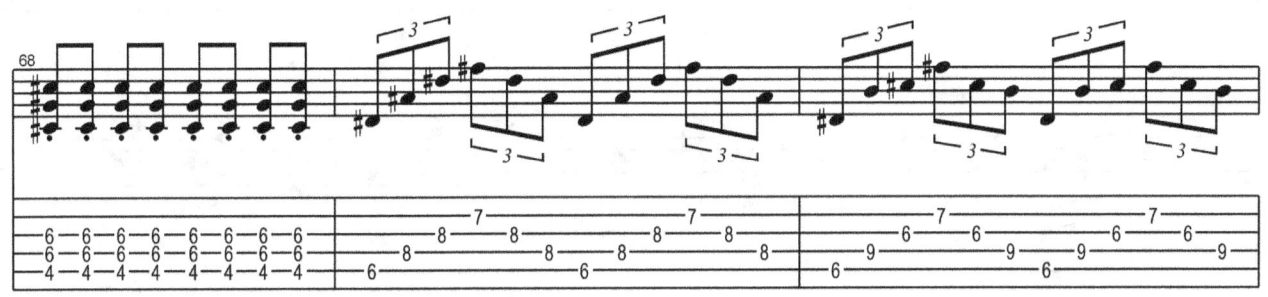
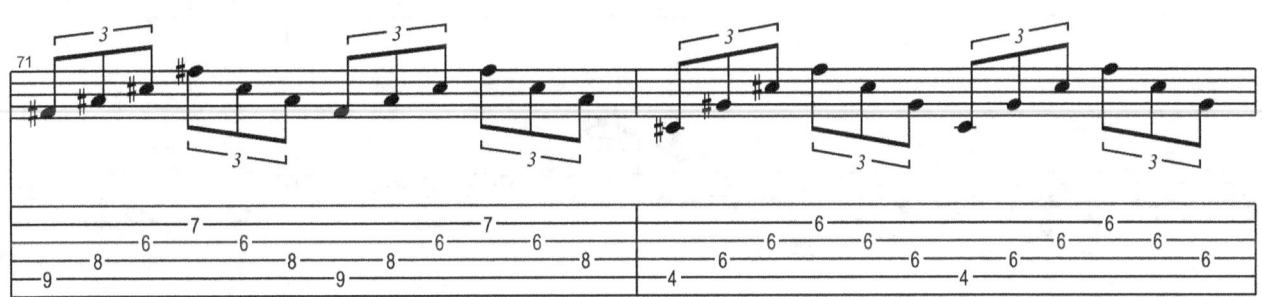
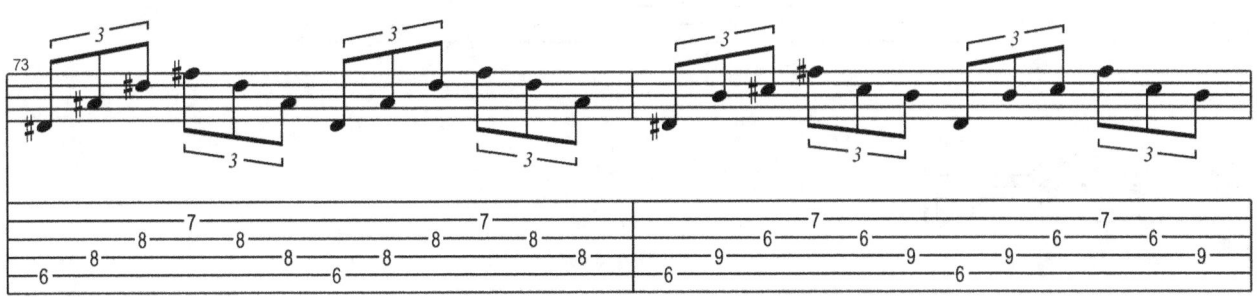

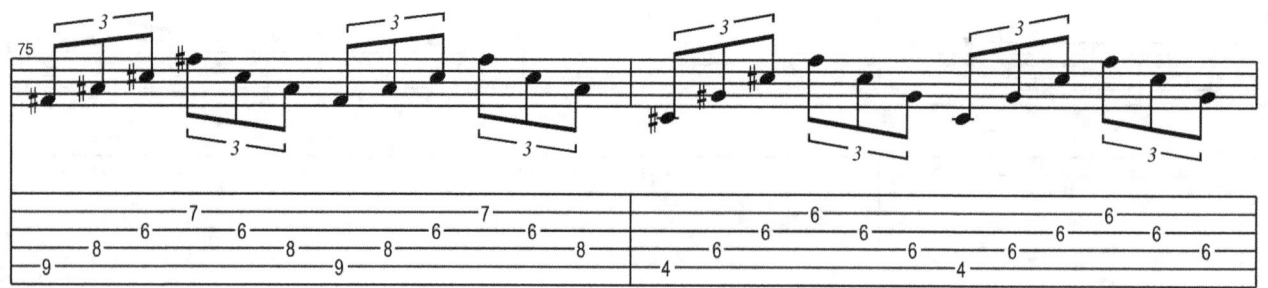
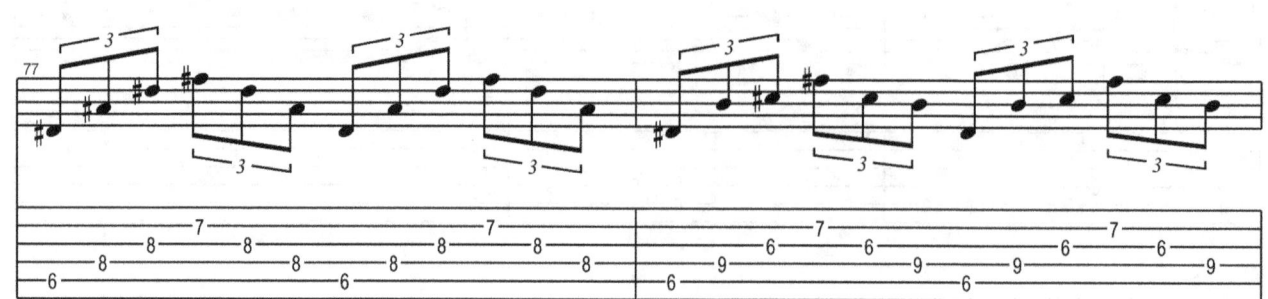
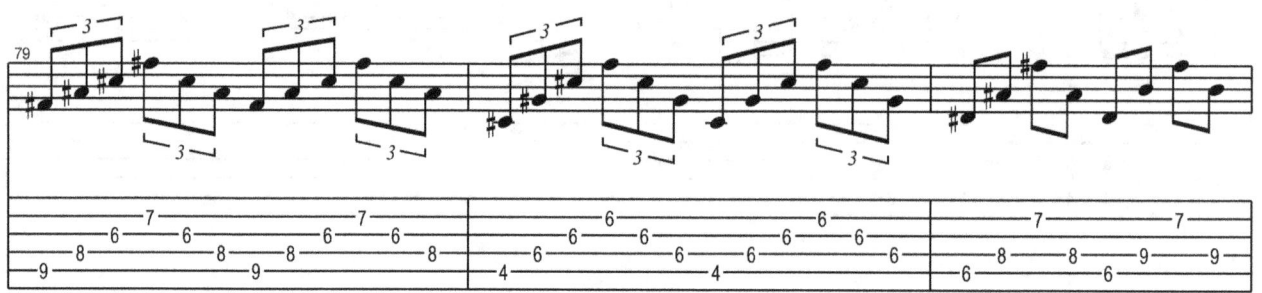
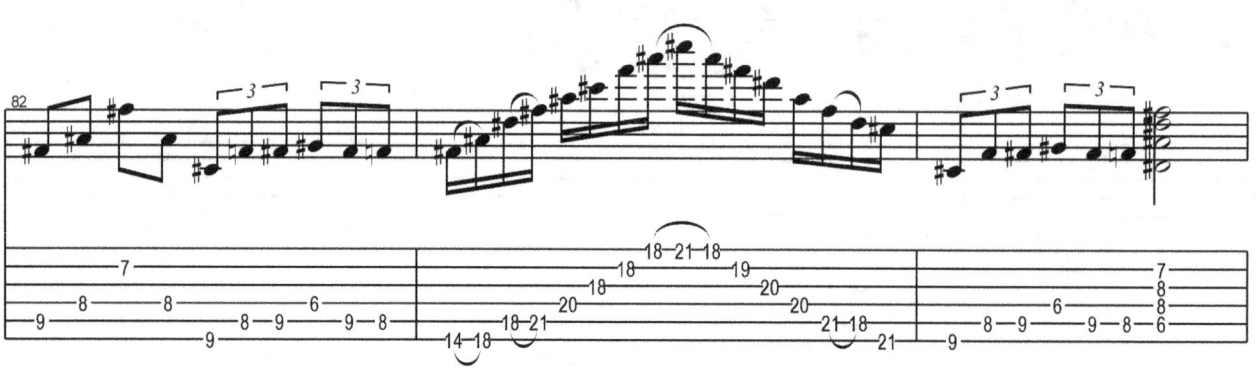
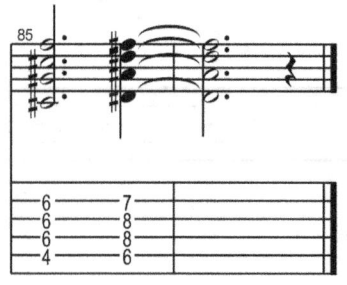

"Only Dust Remains"
Guitar 2

Music by Matej Sack

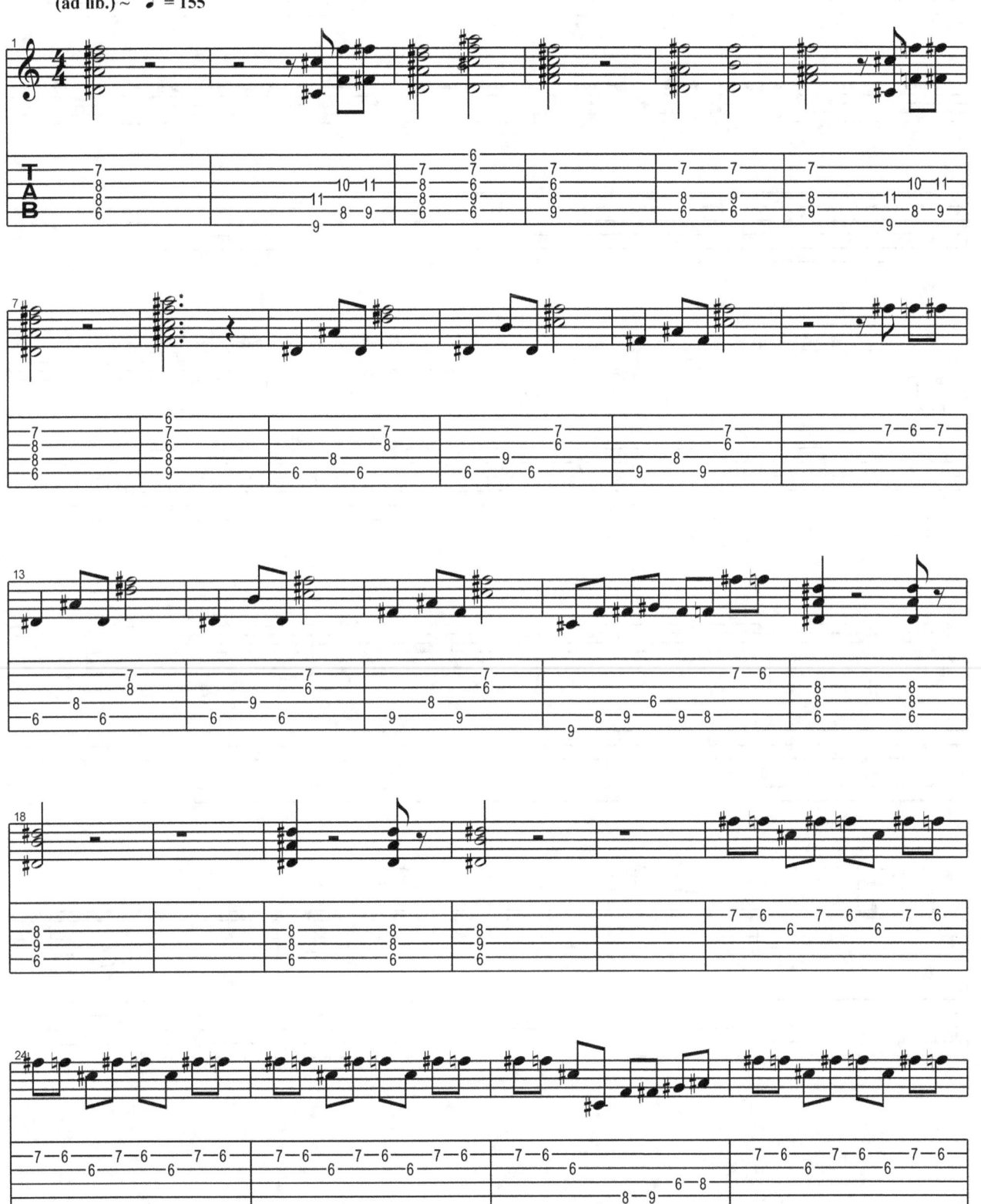

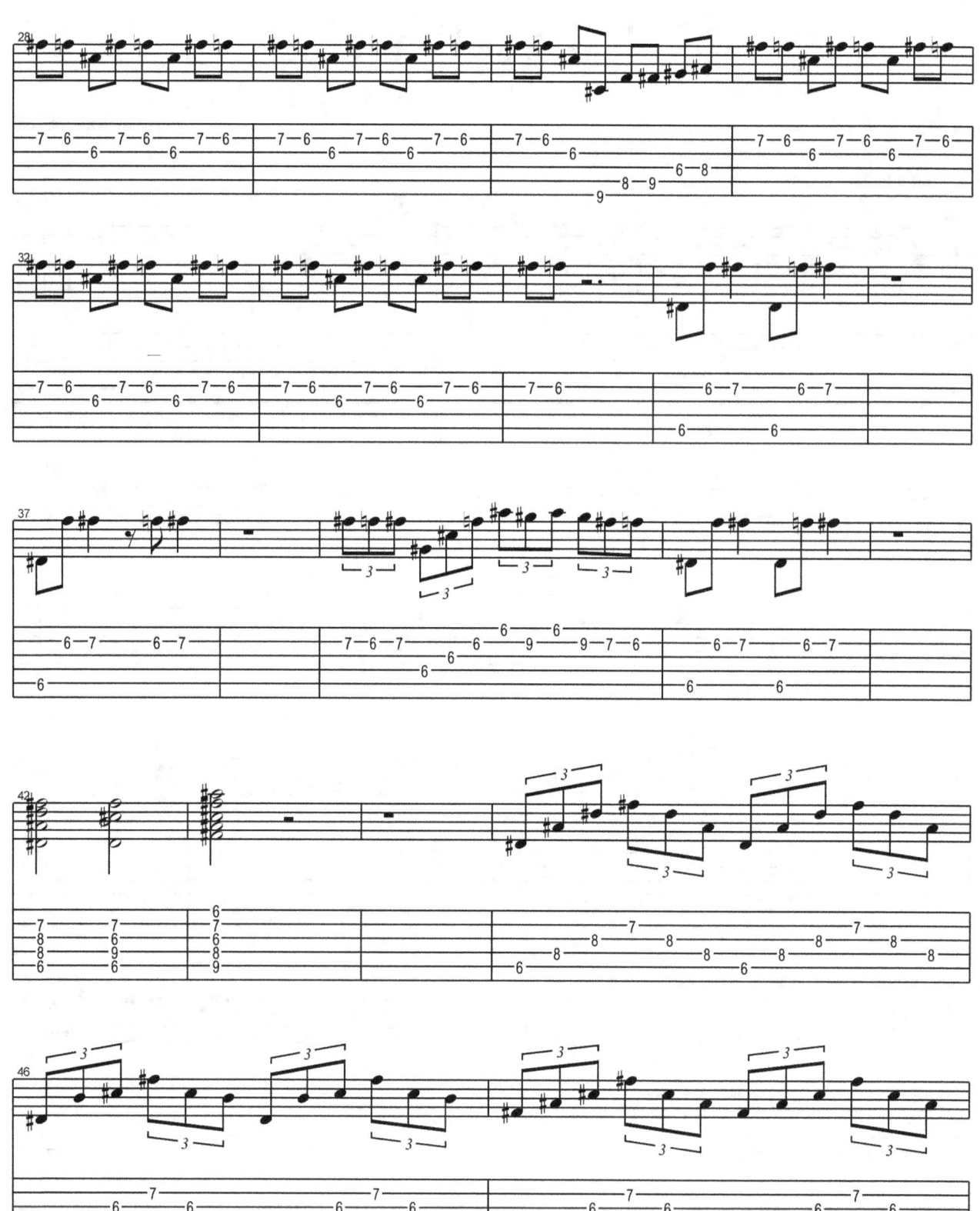

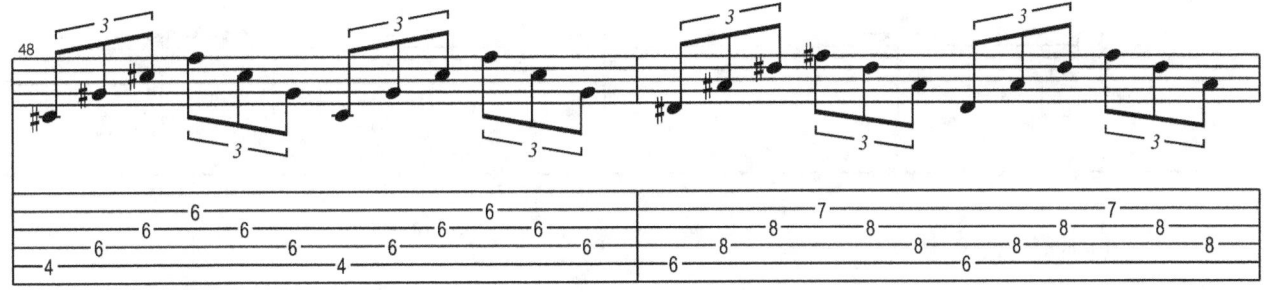
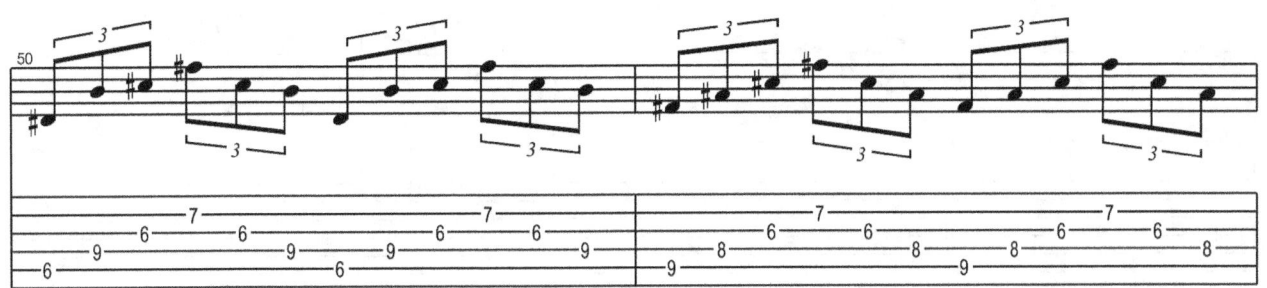
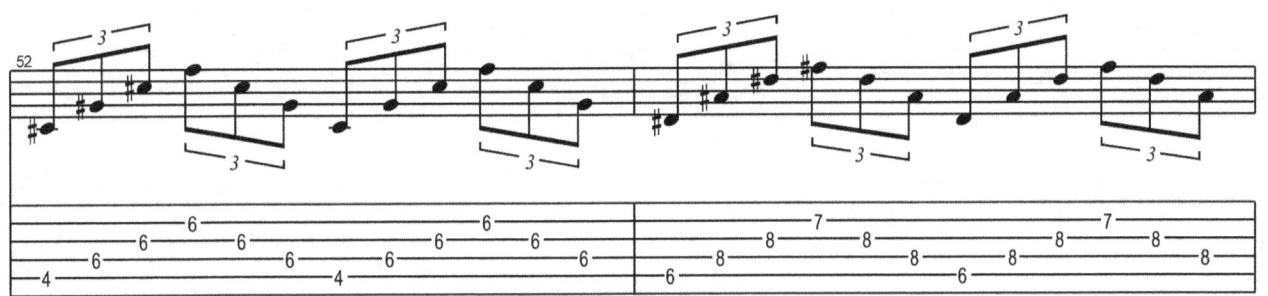
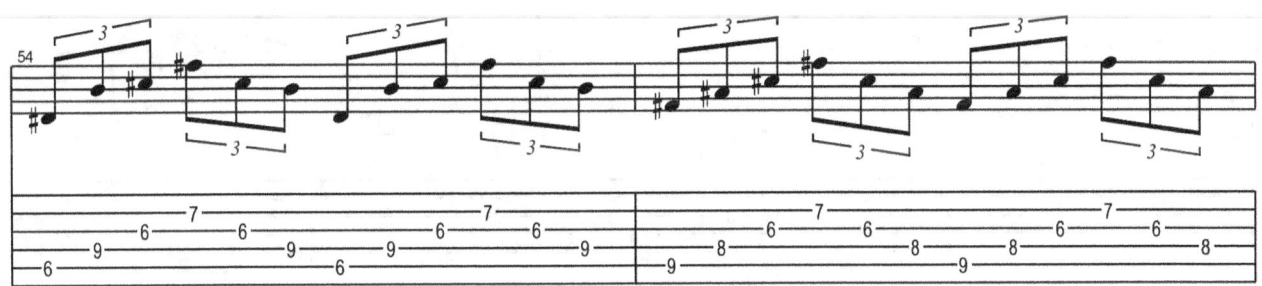
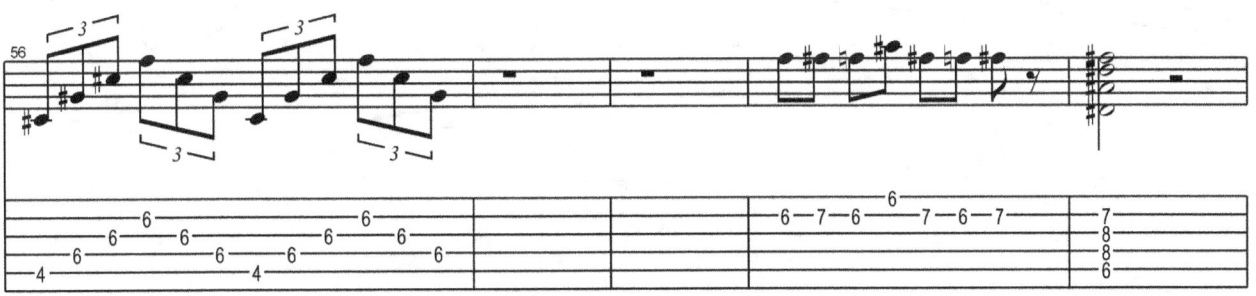

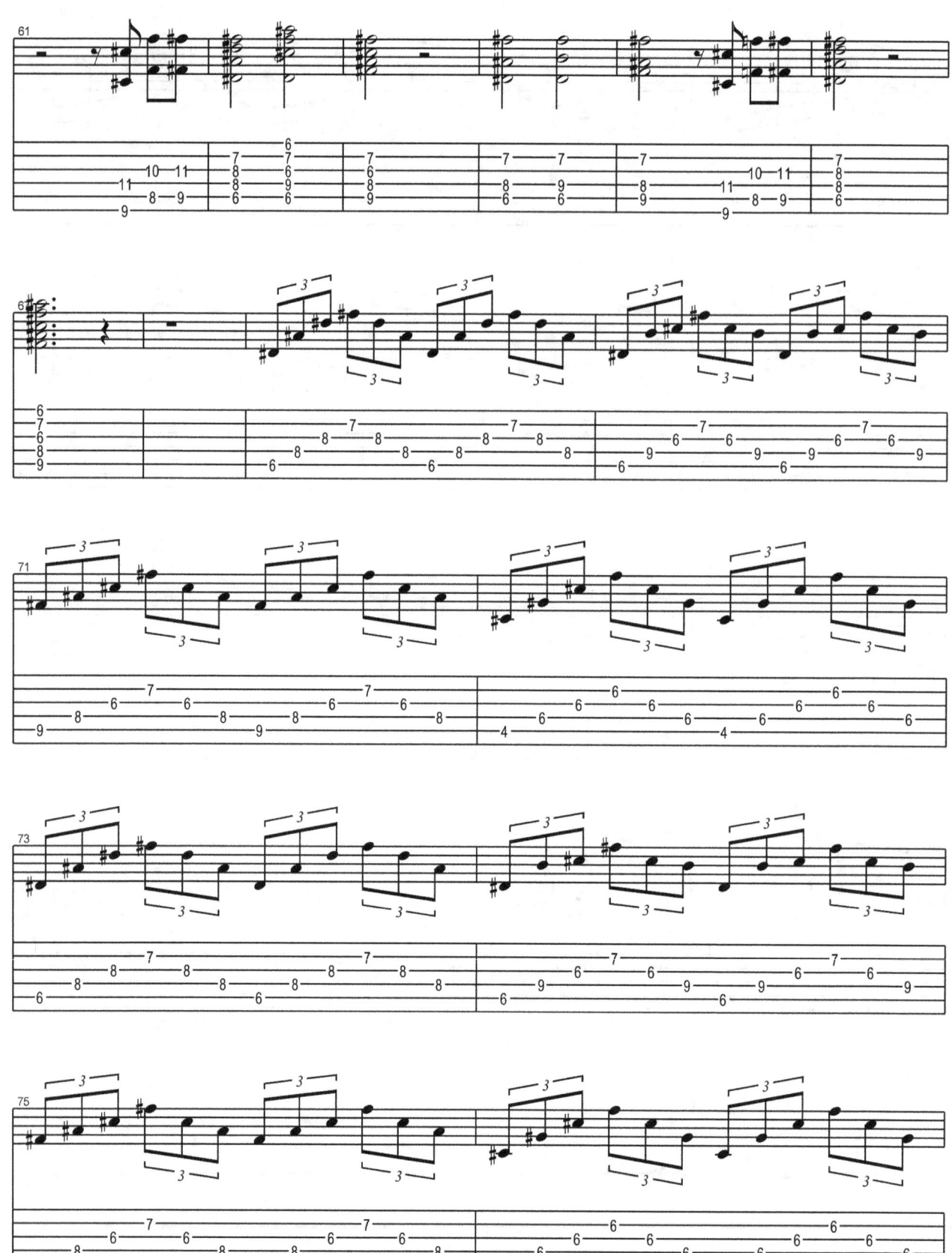

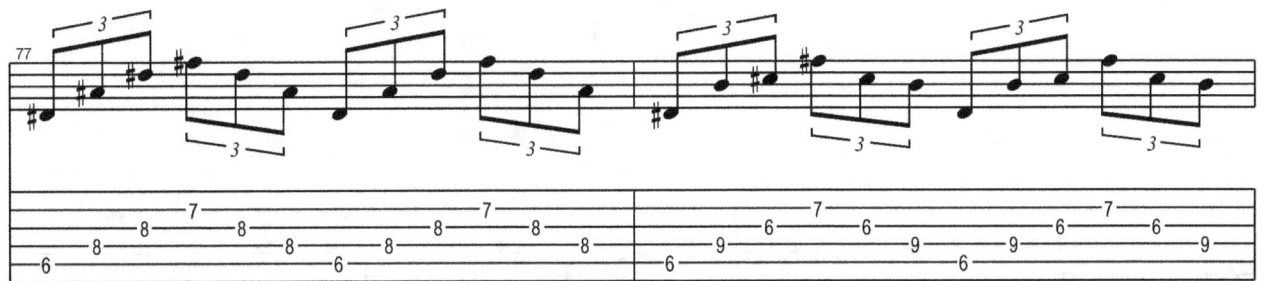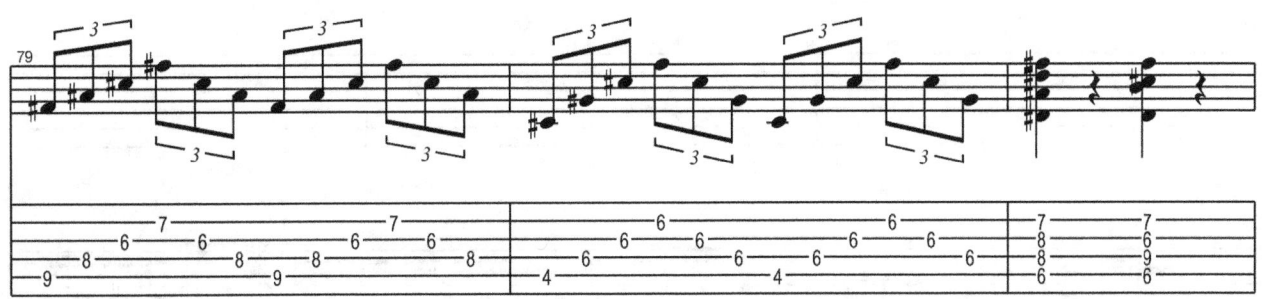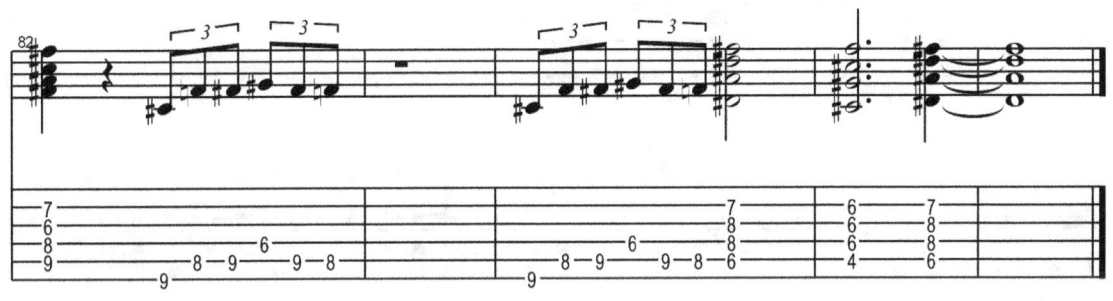

"VII"

Music by Matej Sack

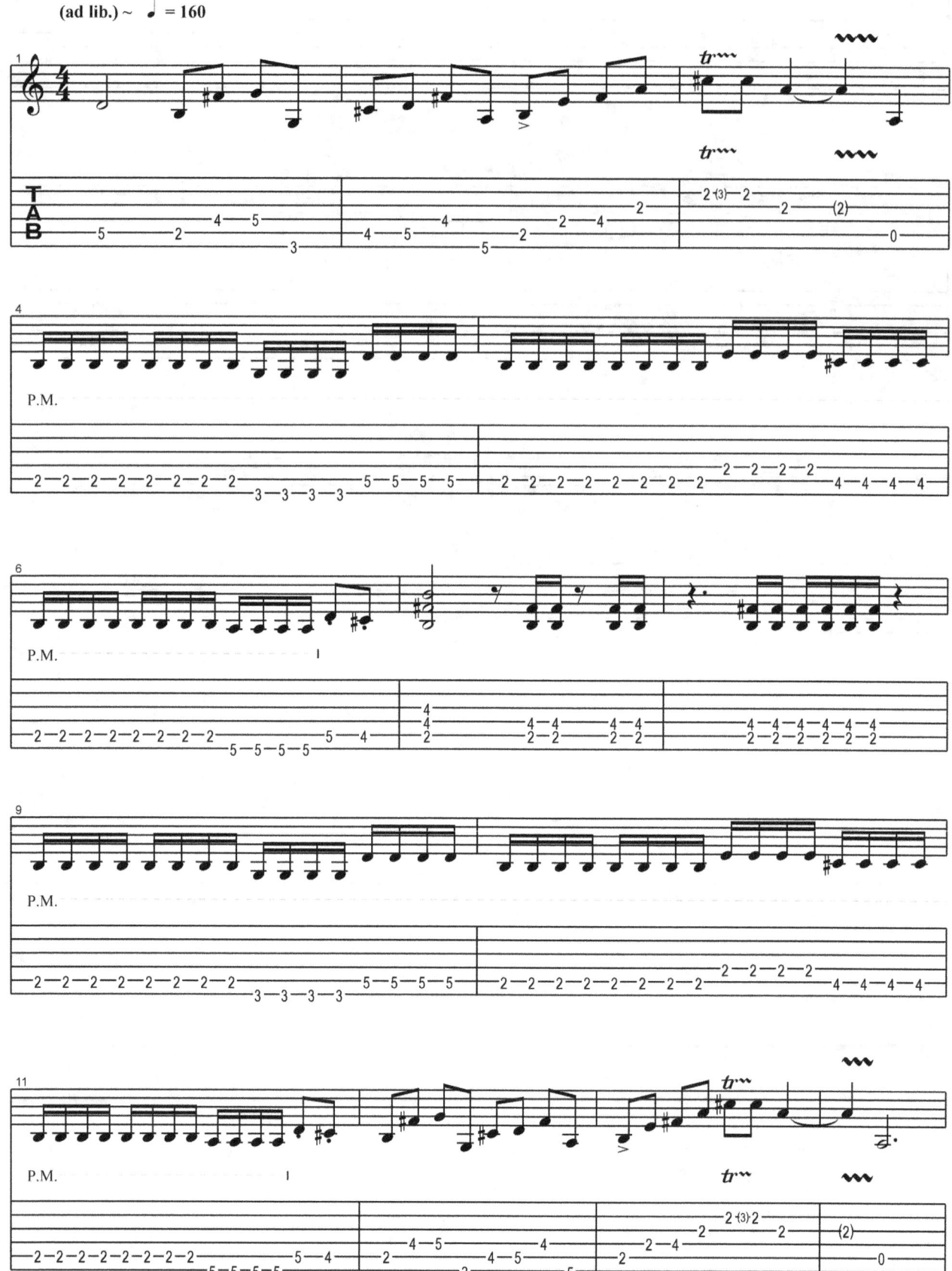

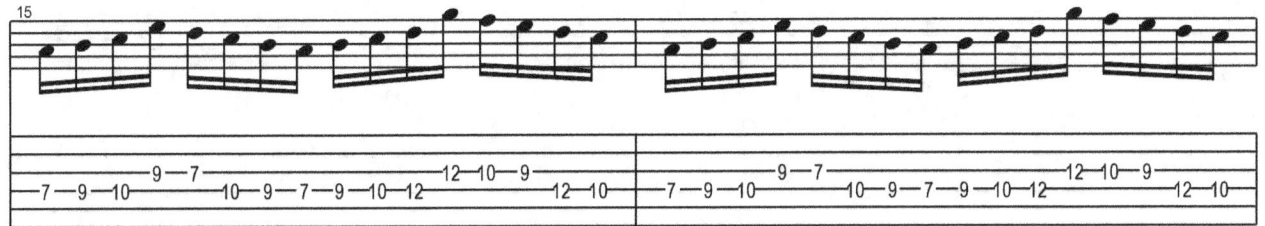
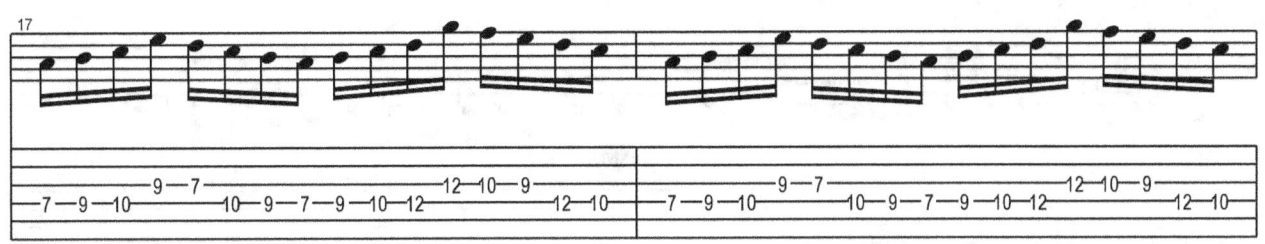
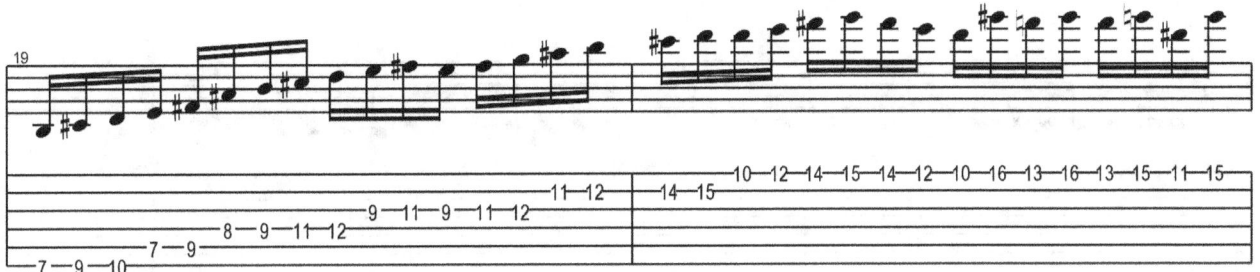
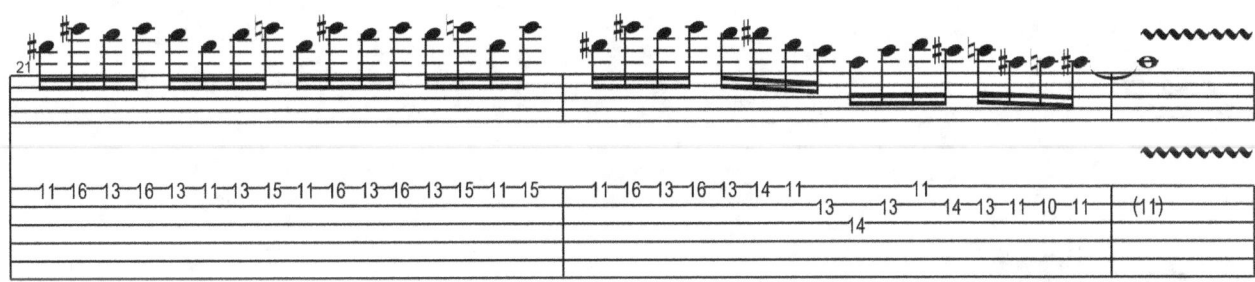
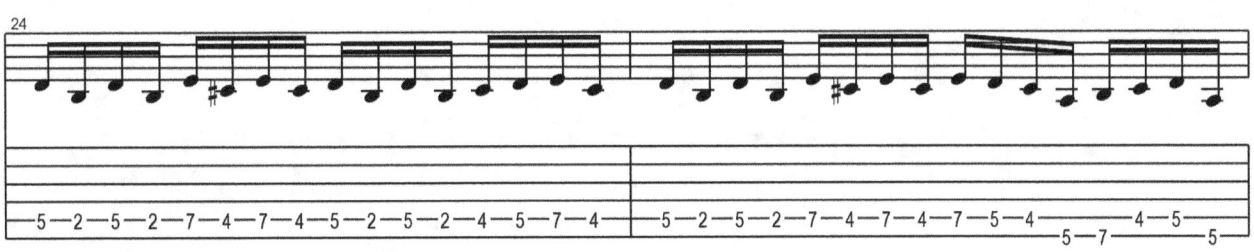
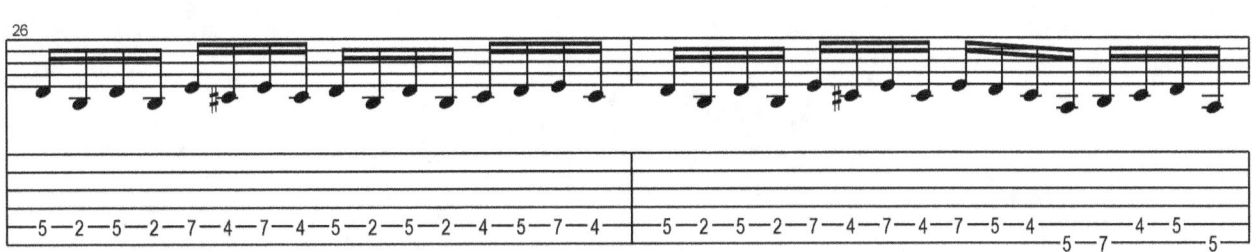

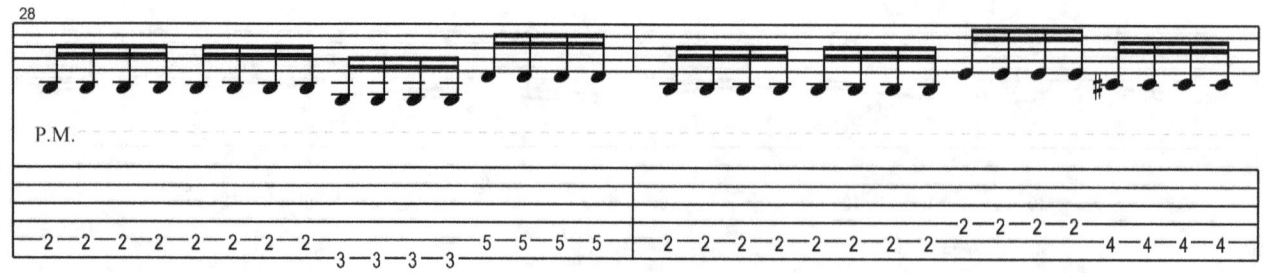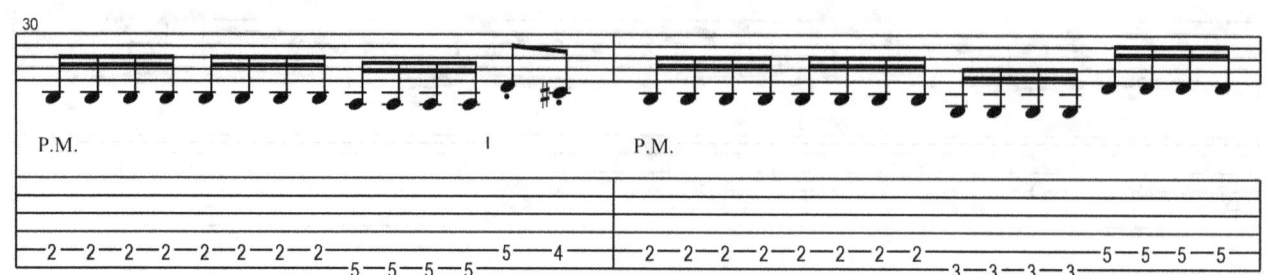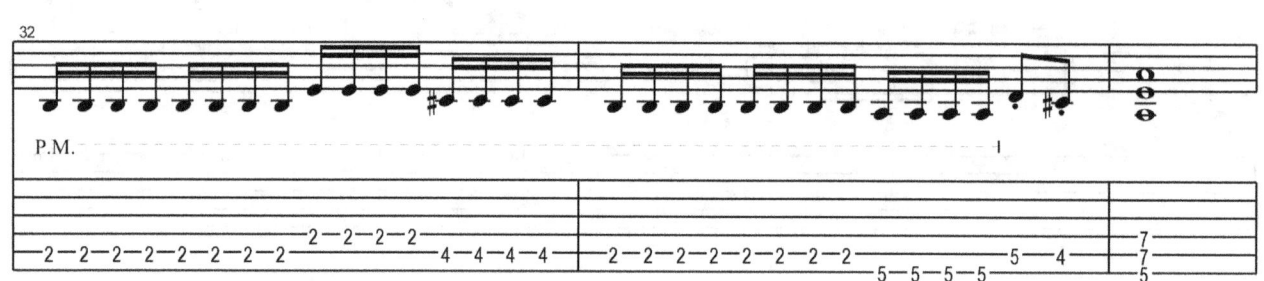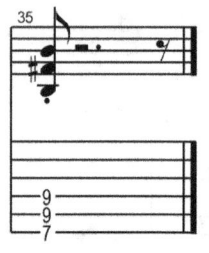

"Legio Solis"

Music by Matej Sack

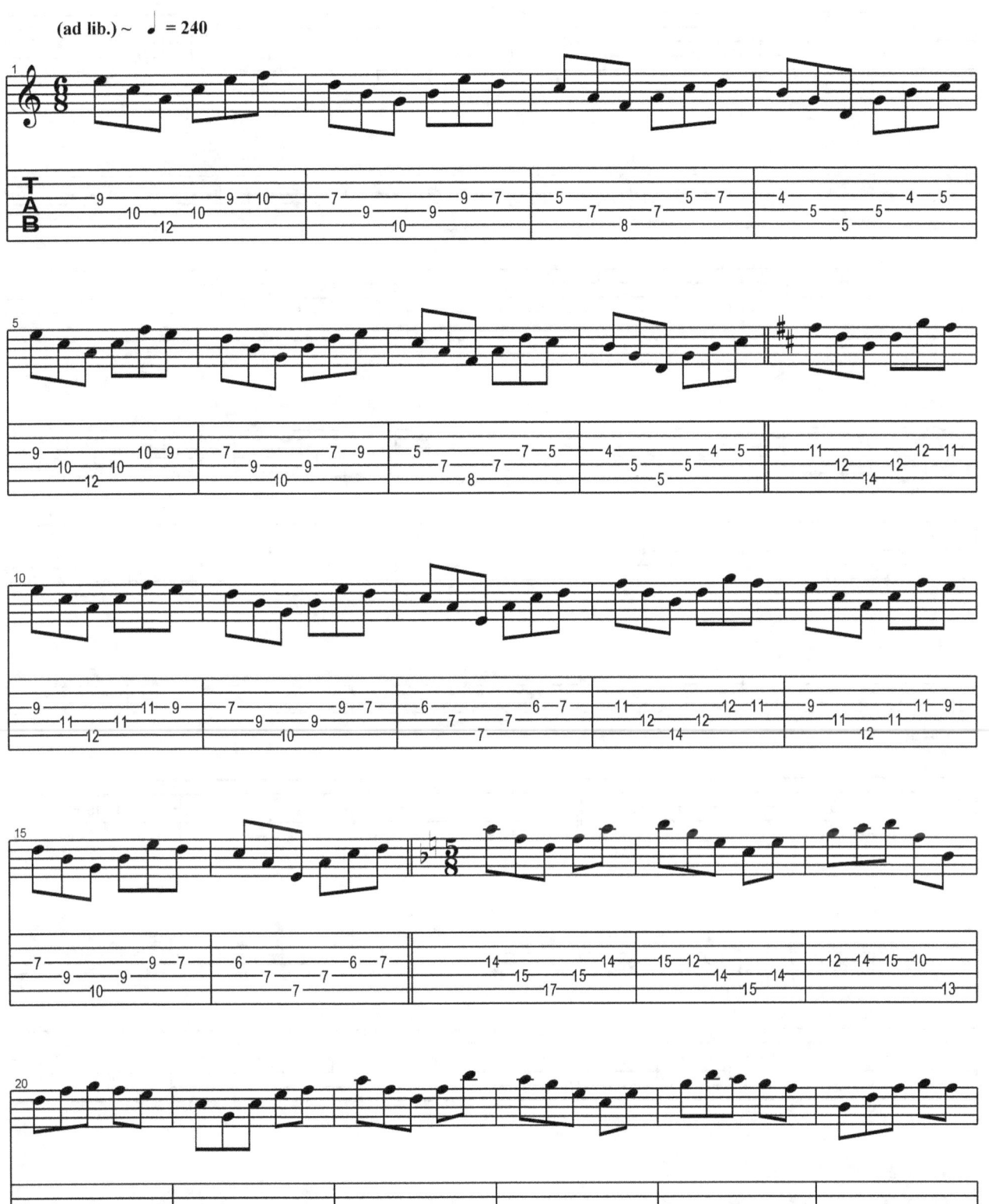

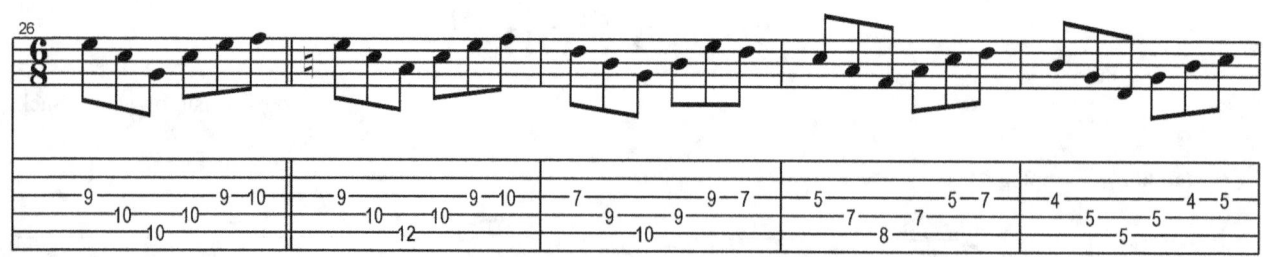
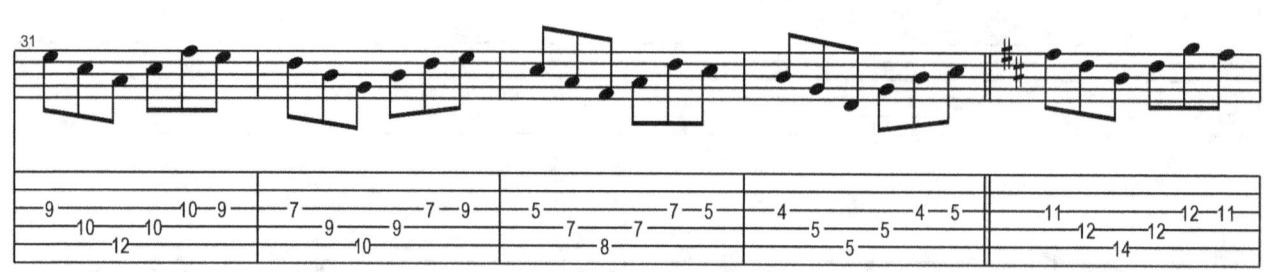
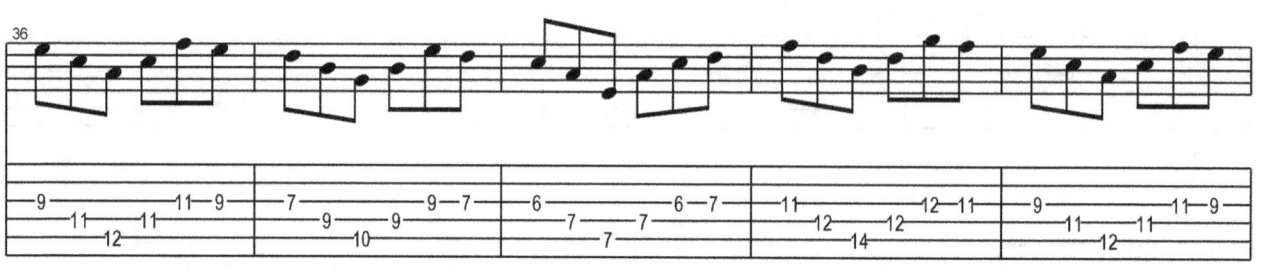
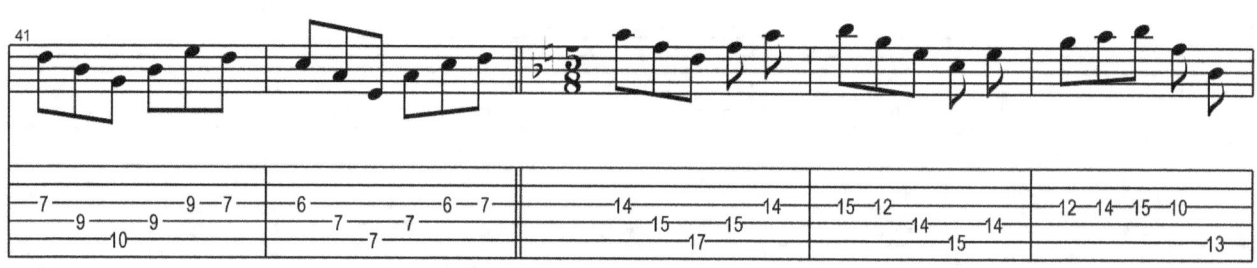
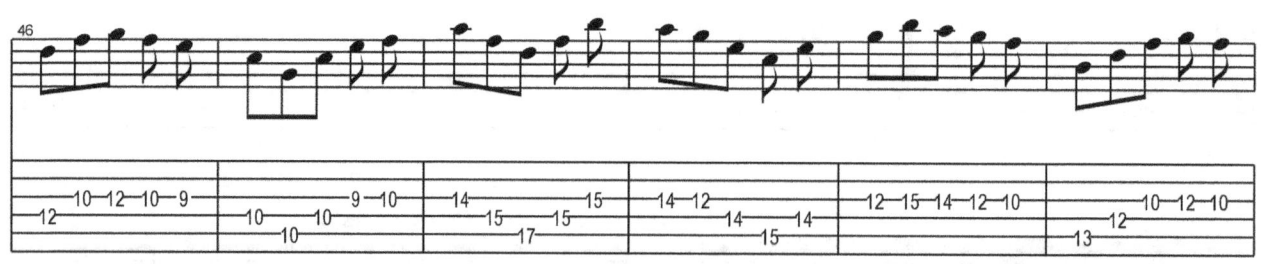
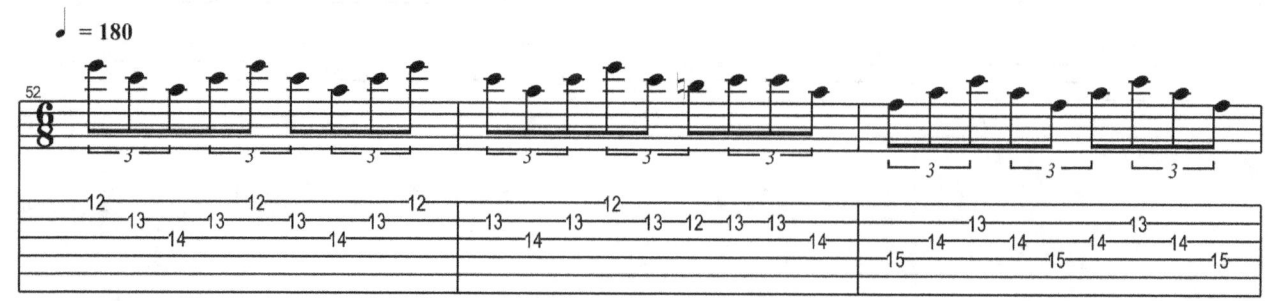

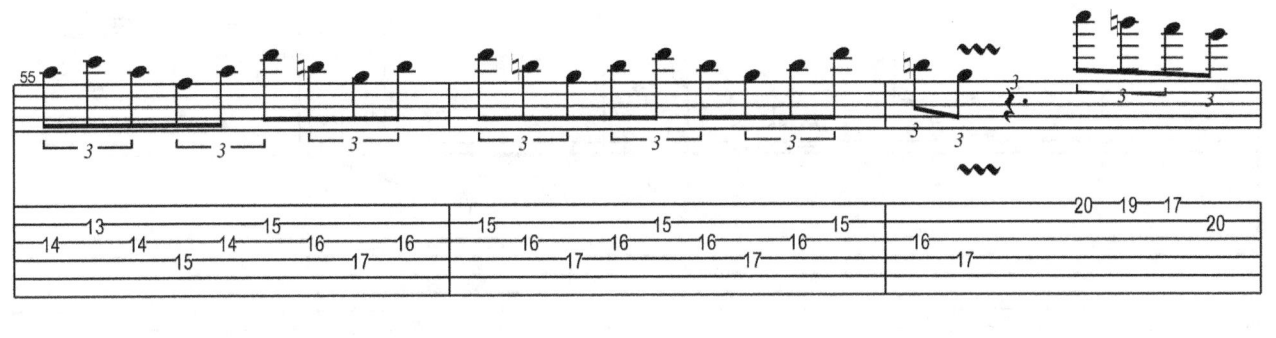
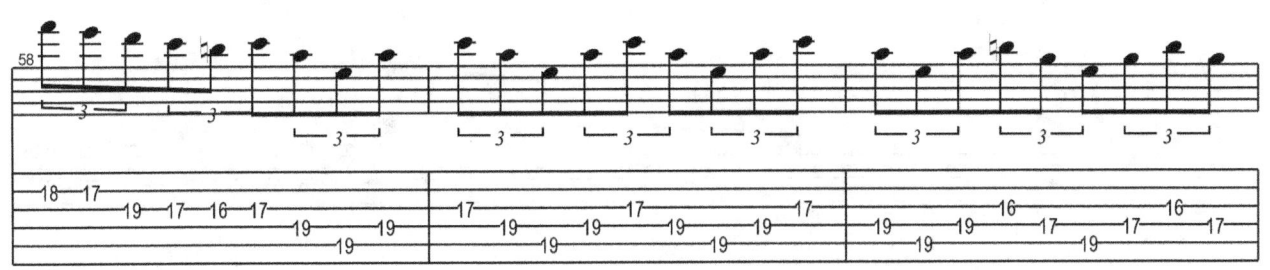
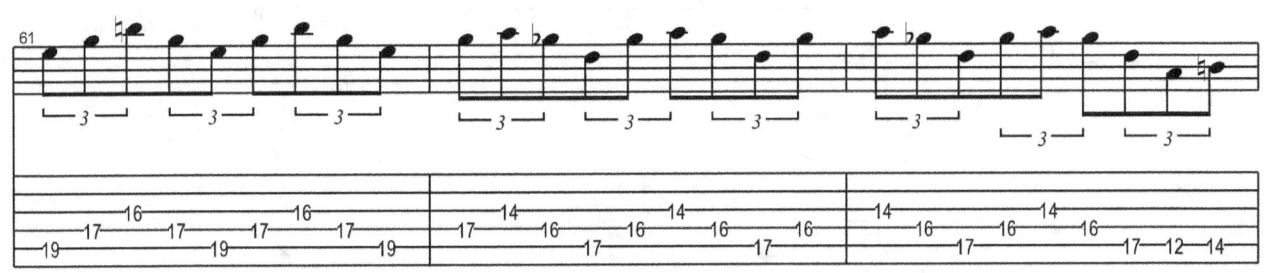
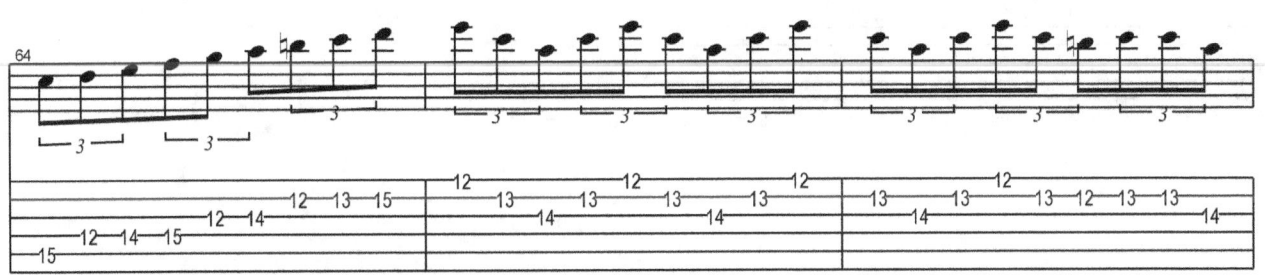
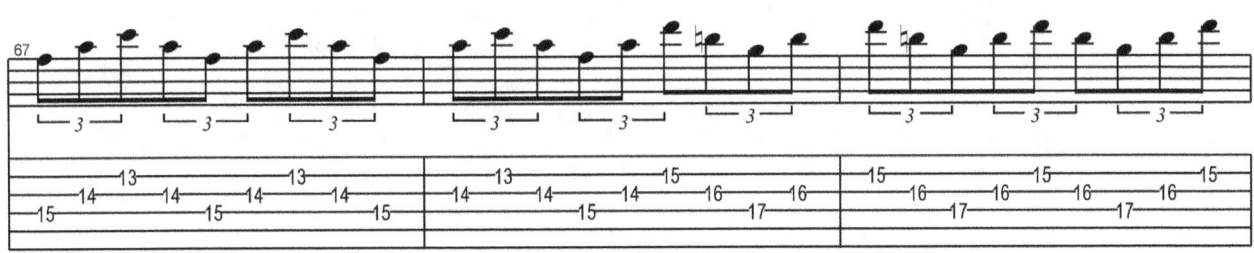

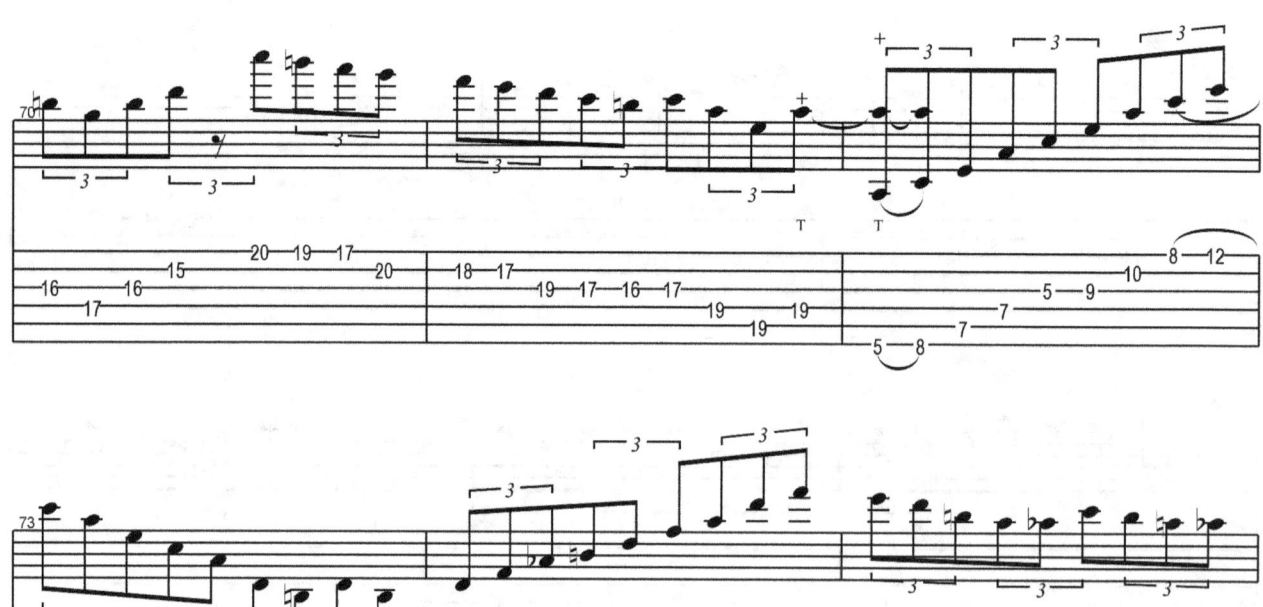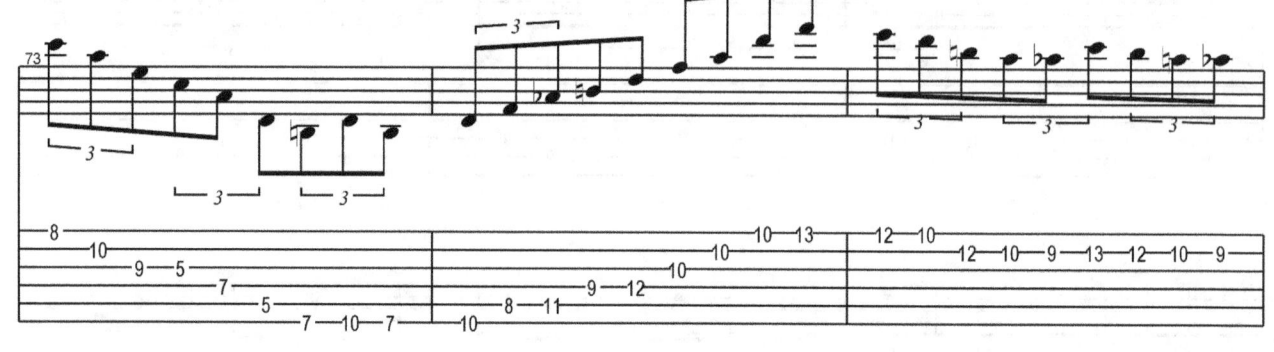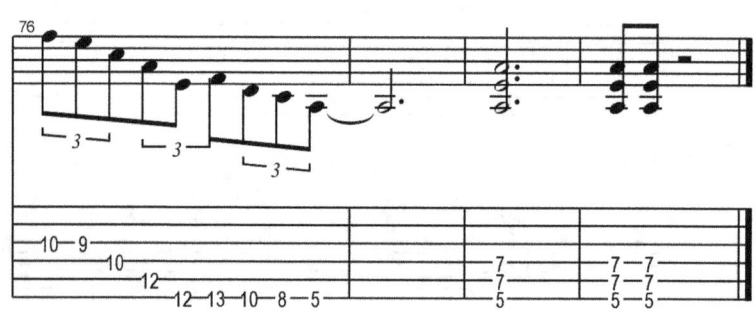

"Will-o'-the-wisp"

Music by Matej Sack

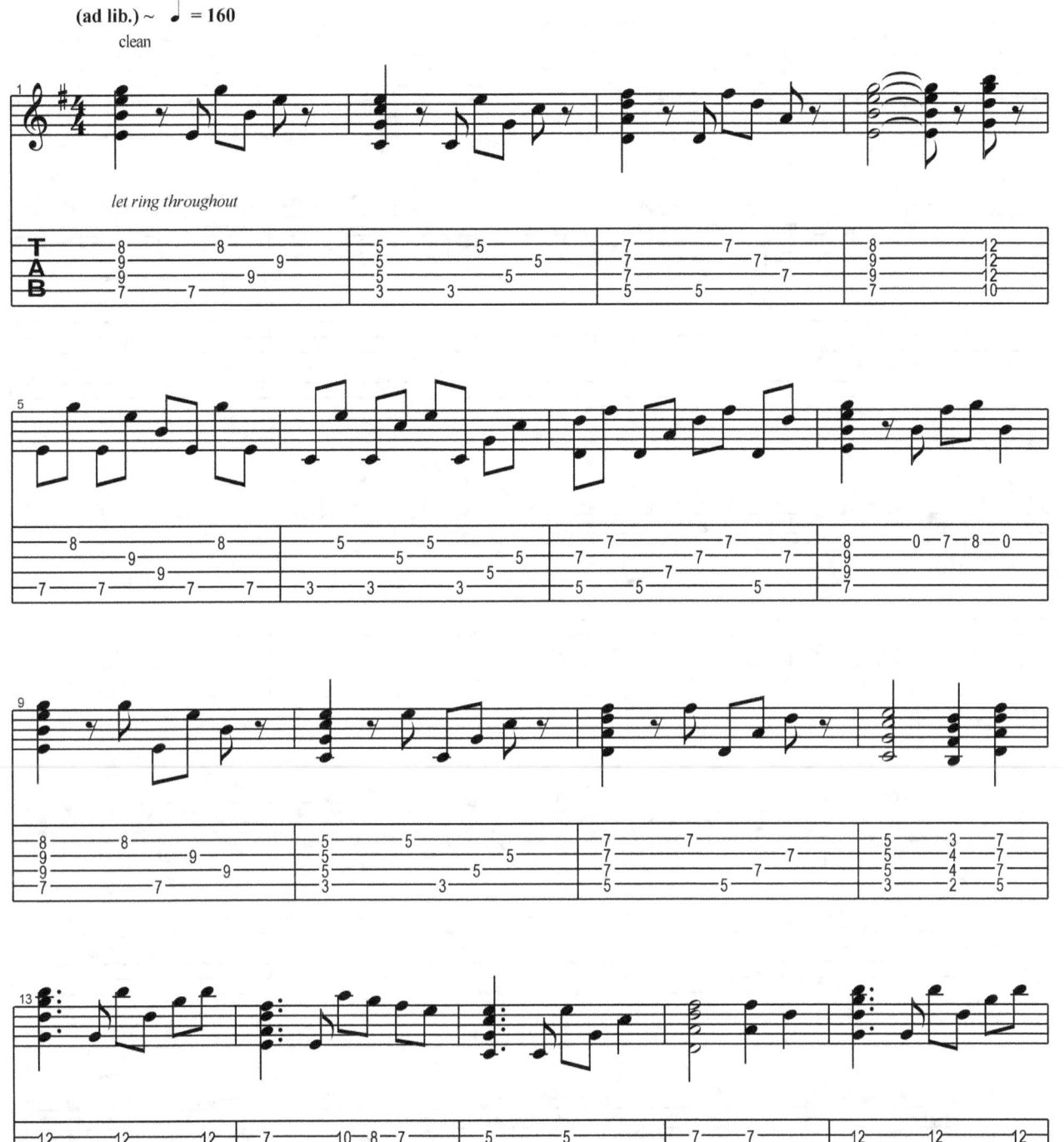

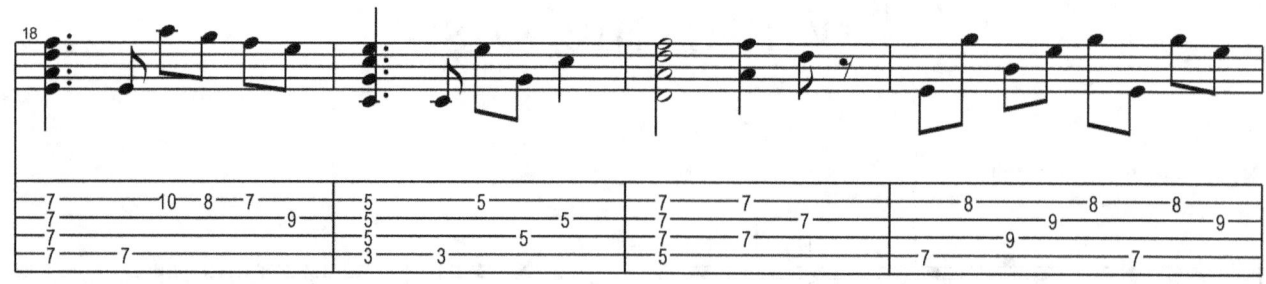
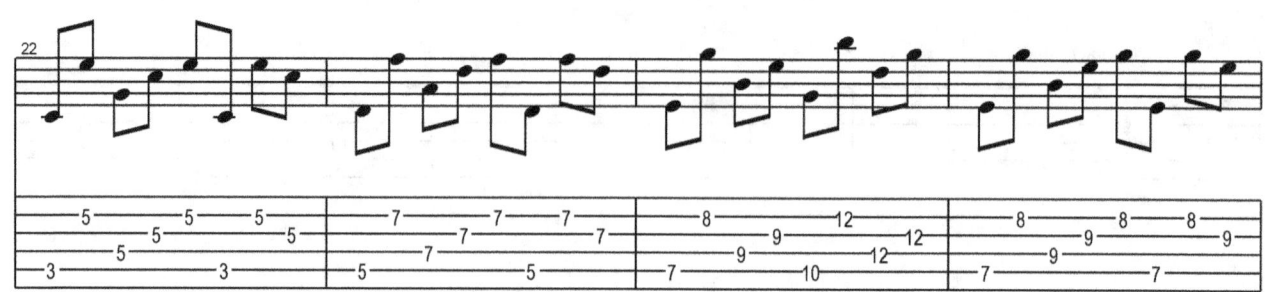
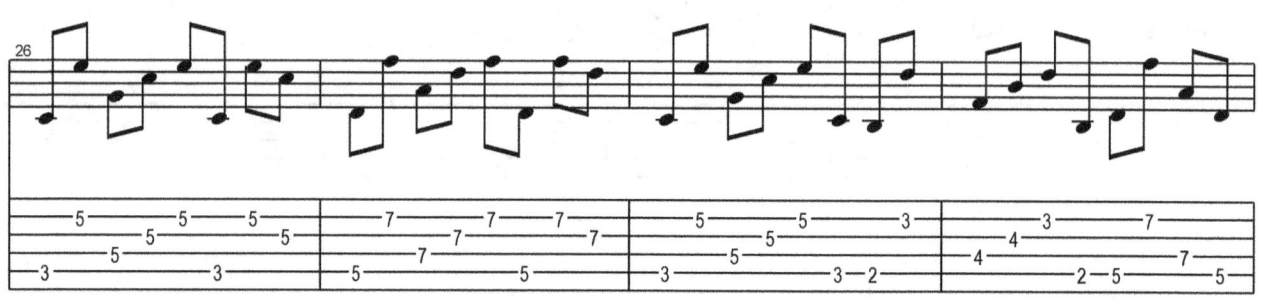
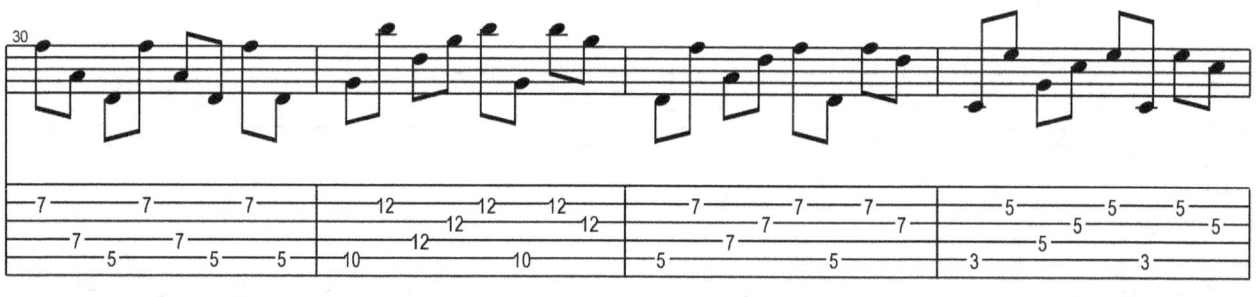
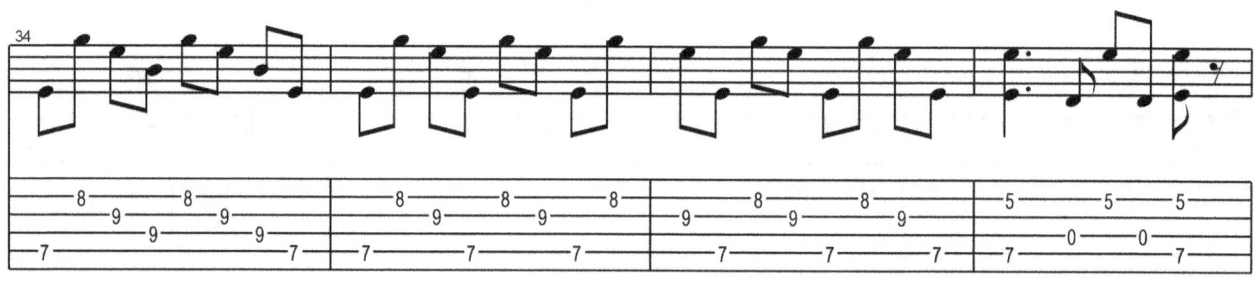

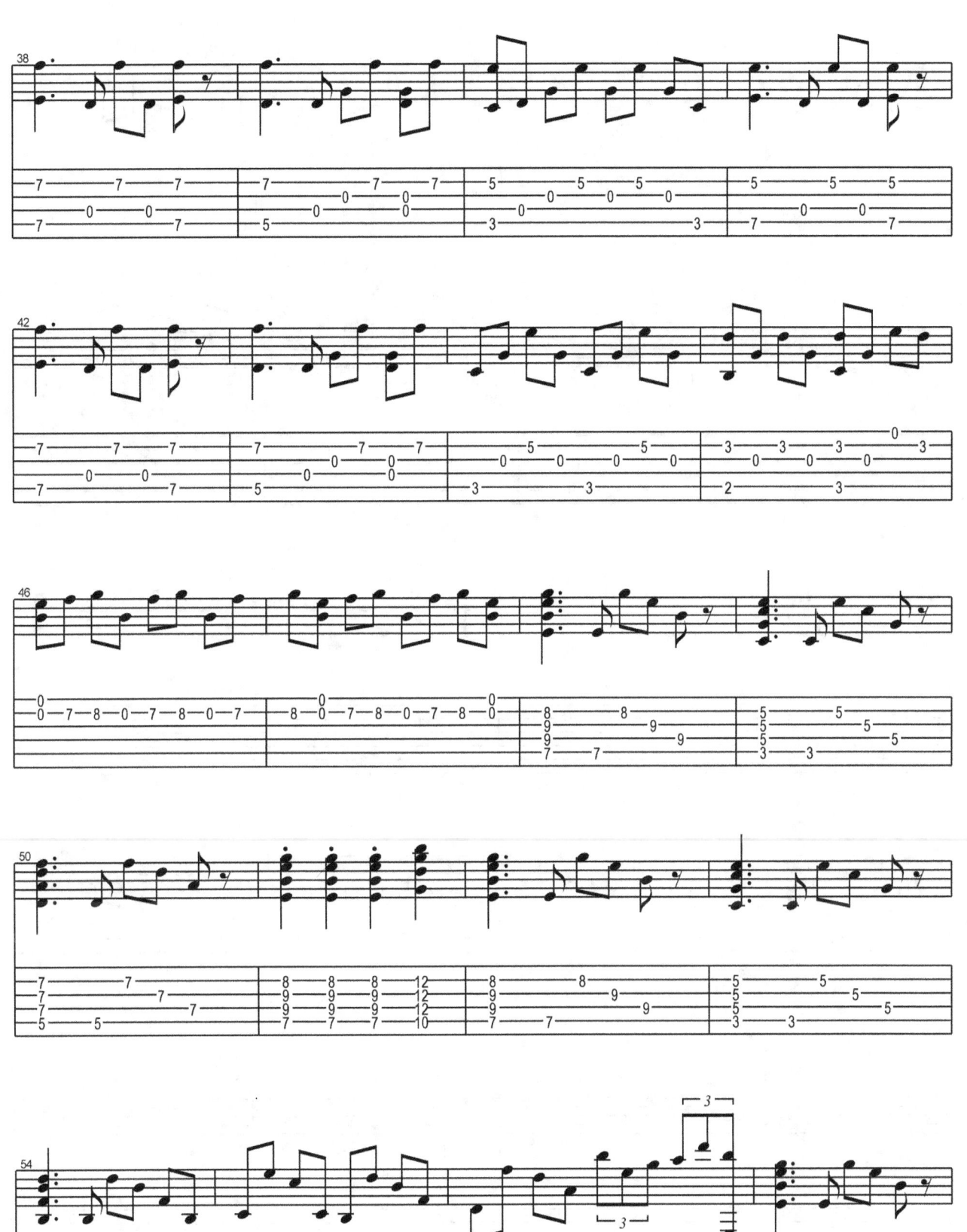

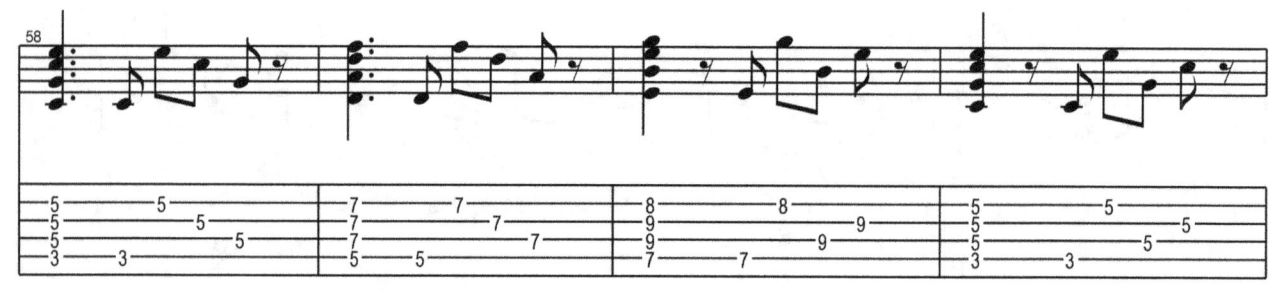
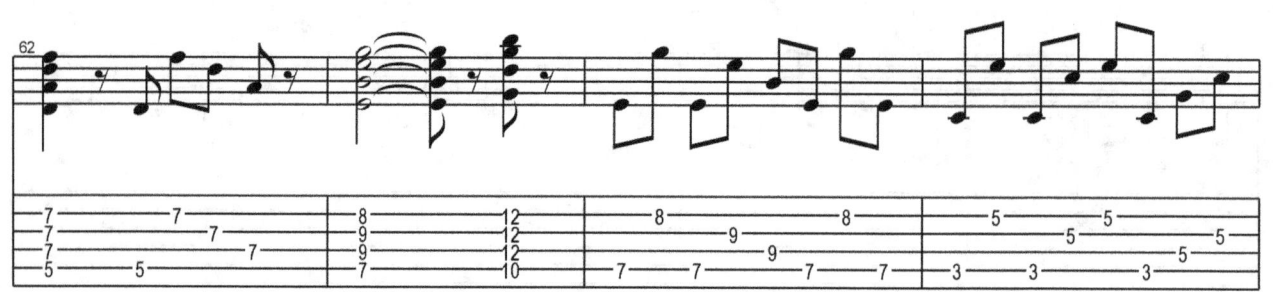
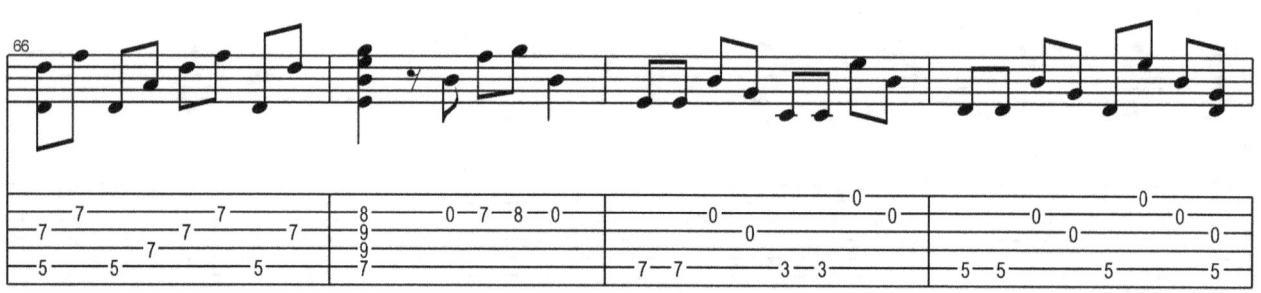
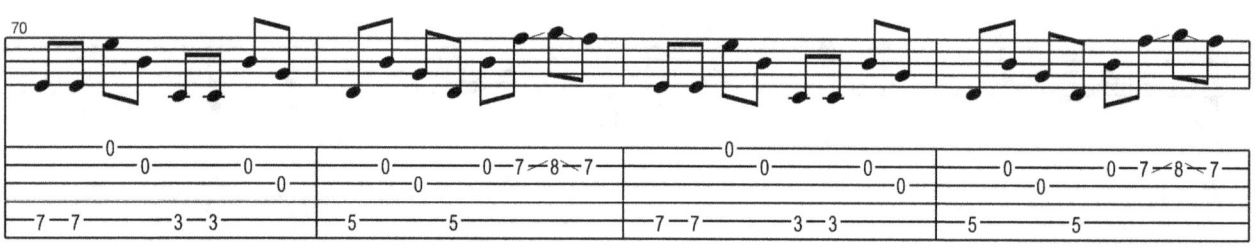
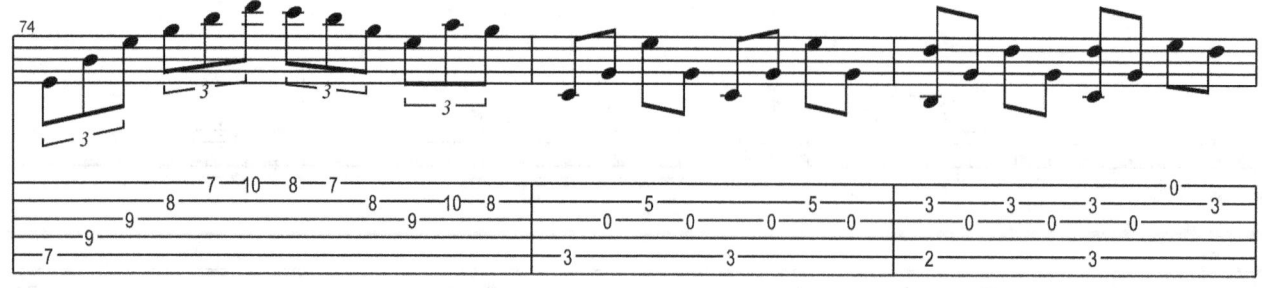

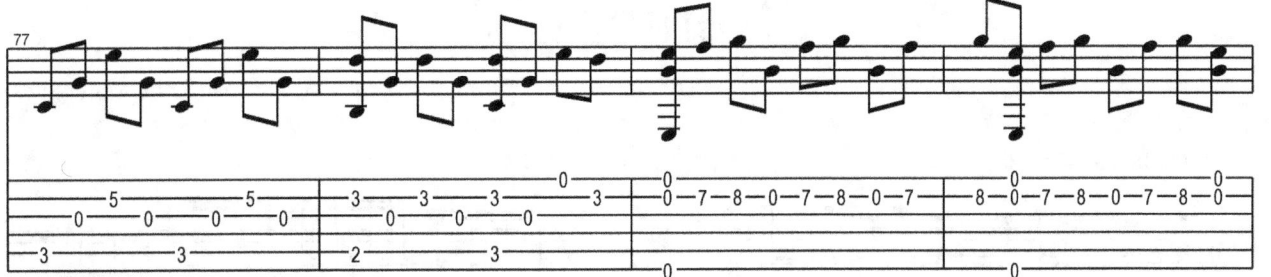
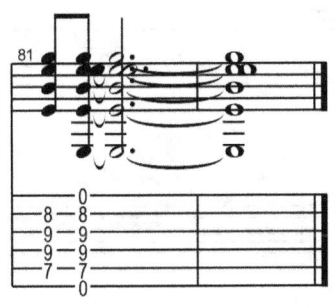

"Nemoralis"

Music by Matej Sack

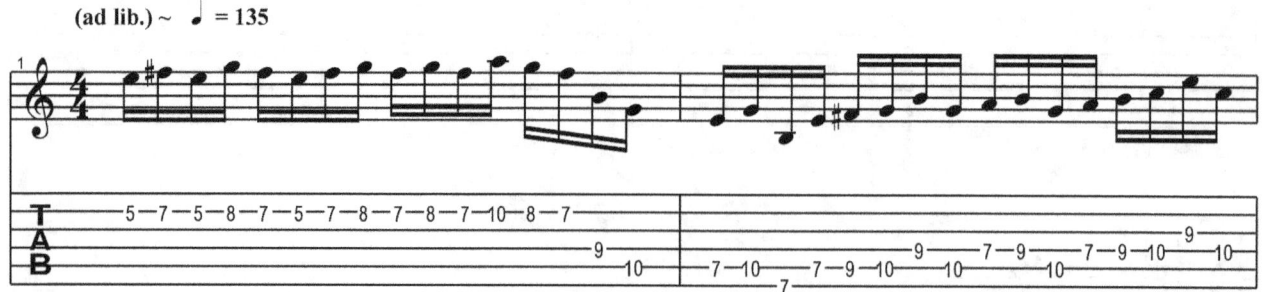
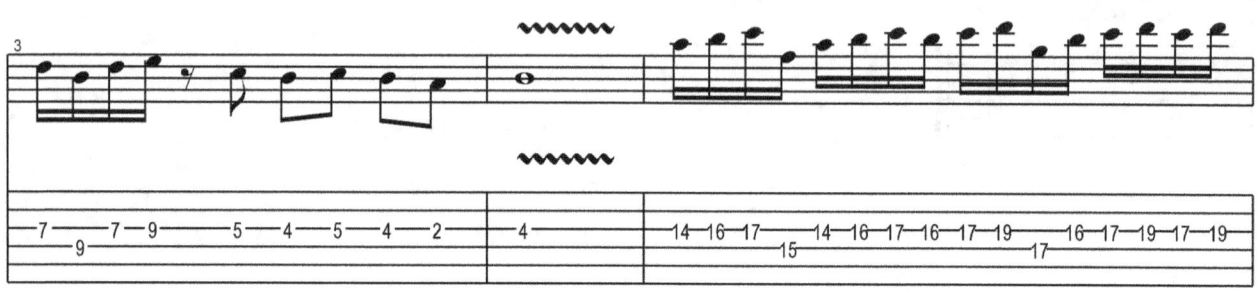
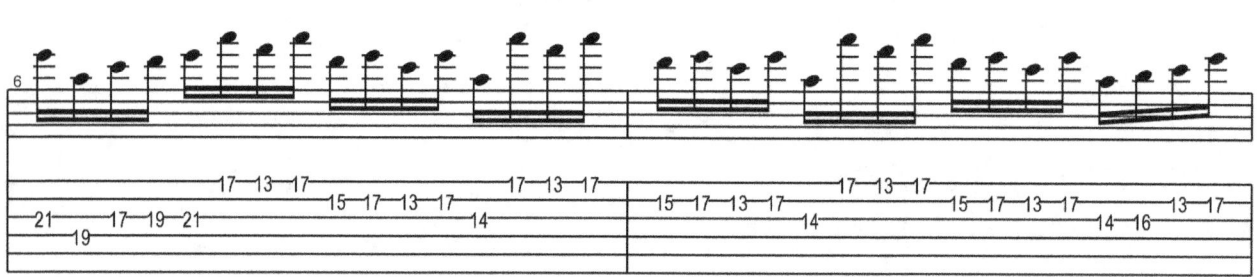
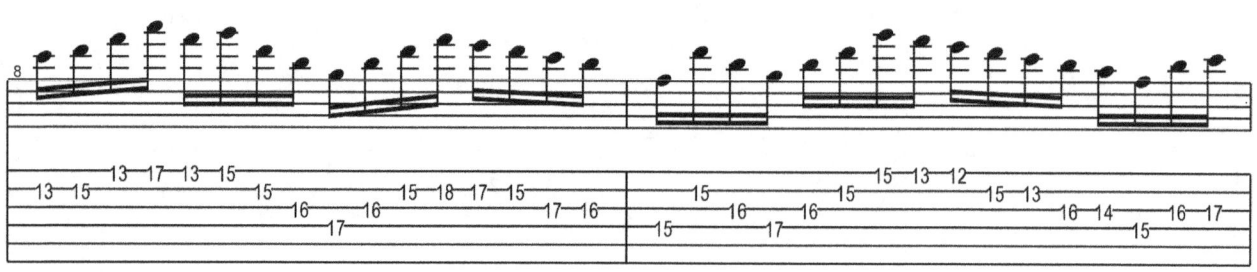
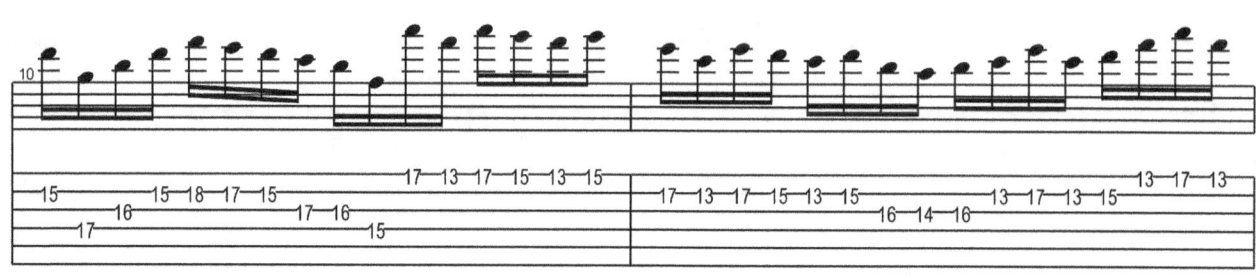

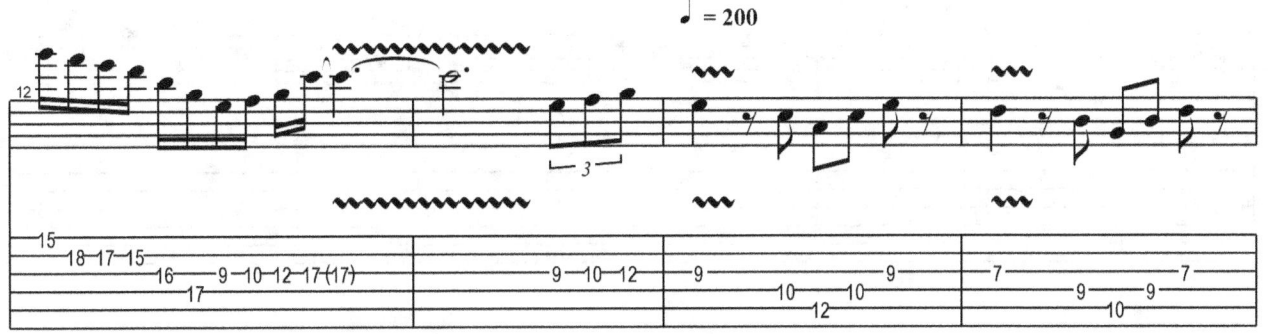
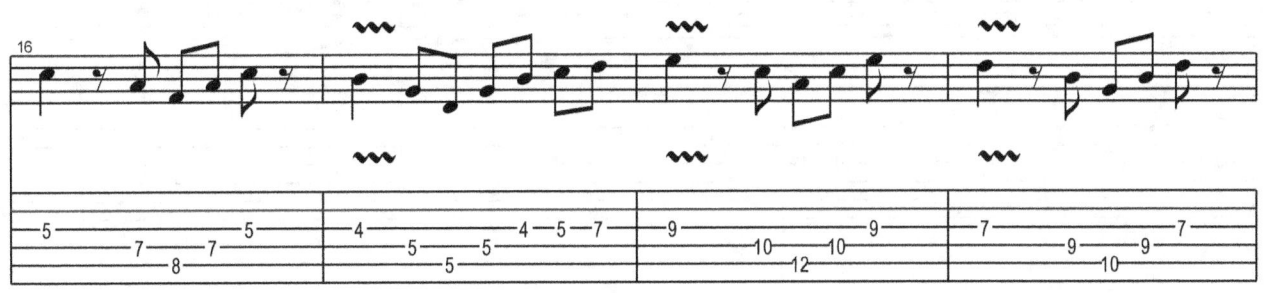
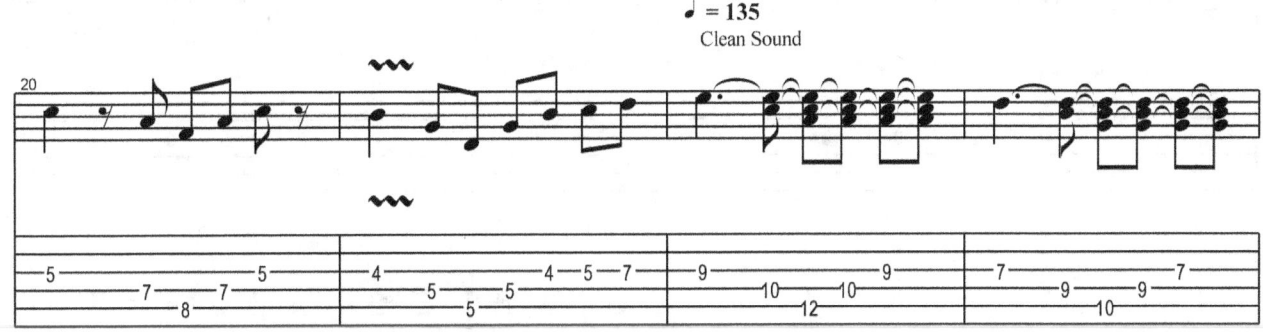
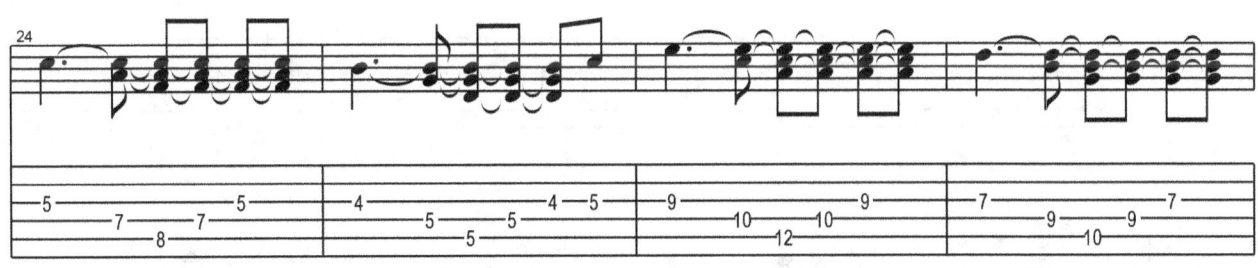
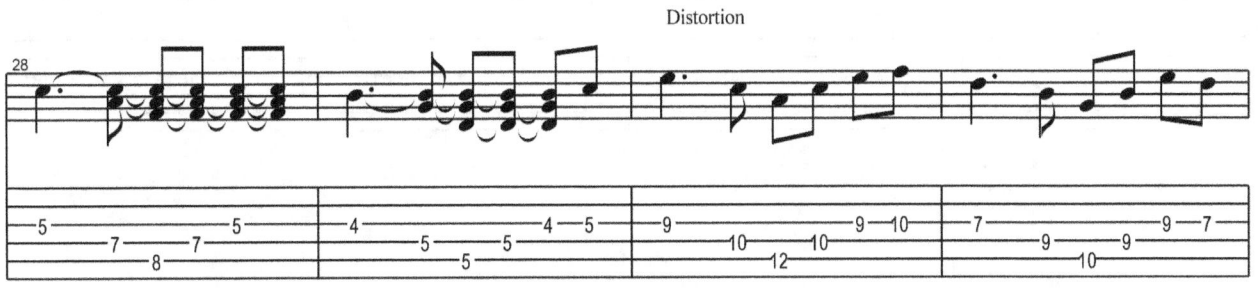

37

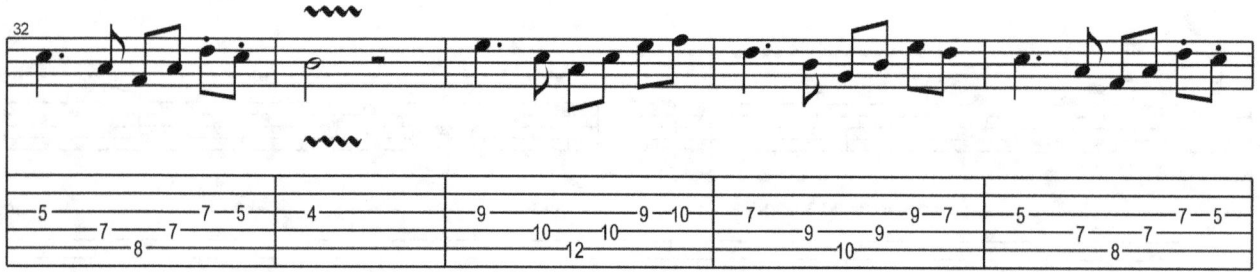
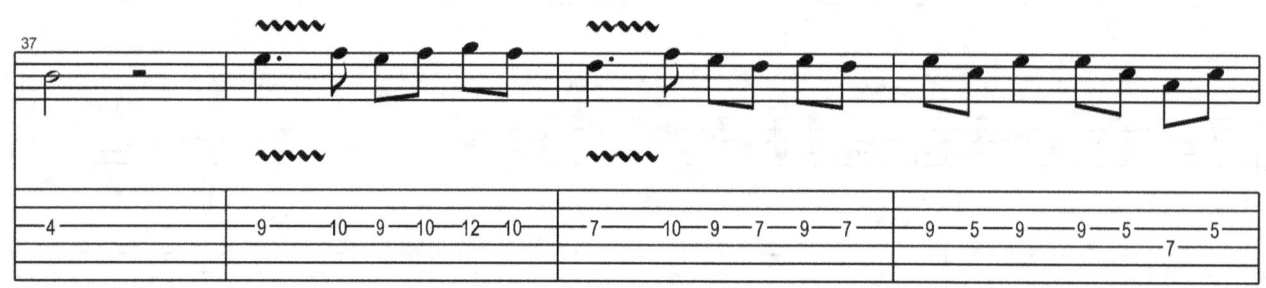
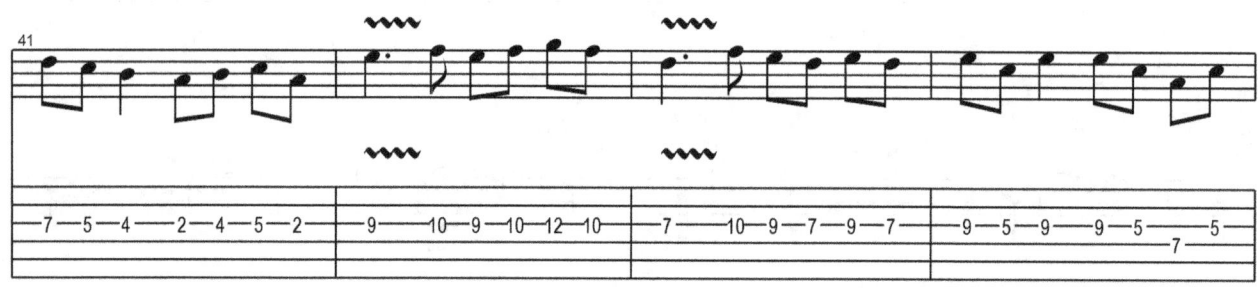
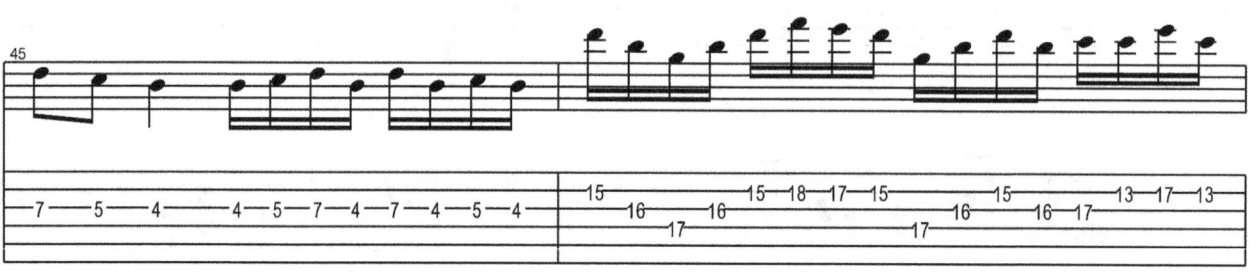
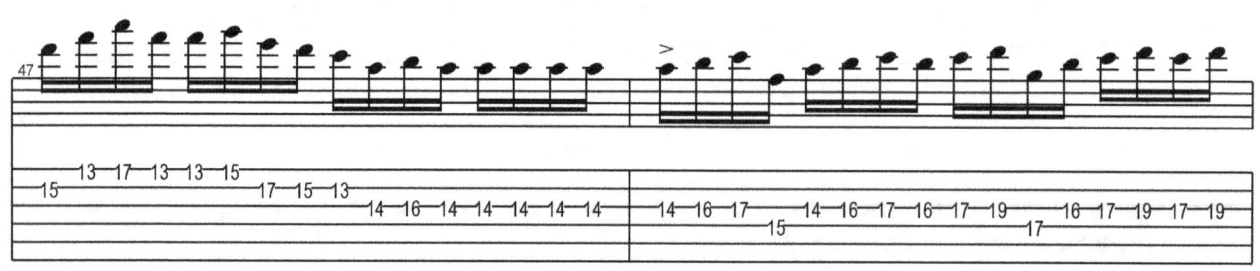

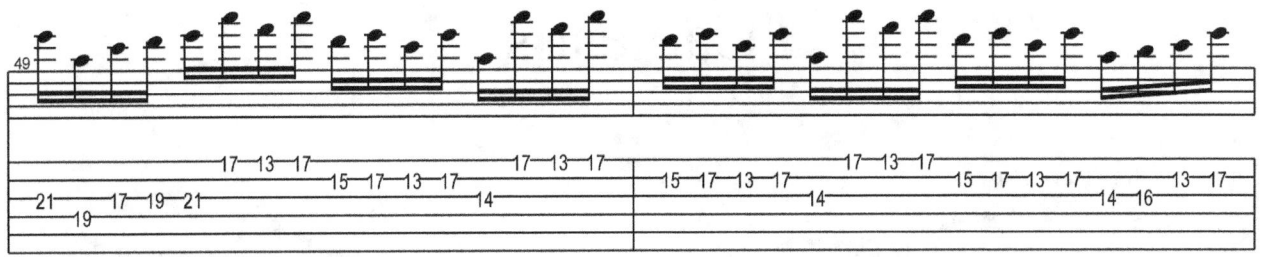
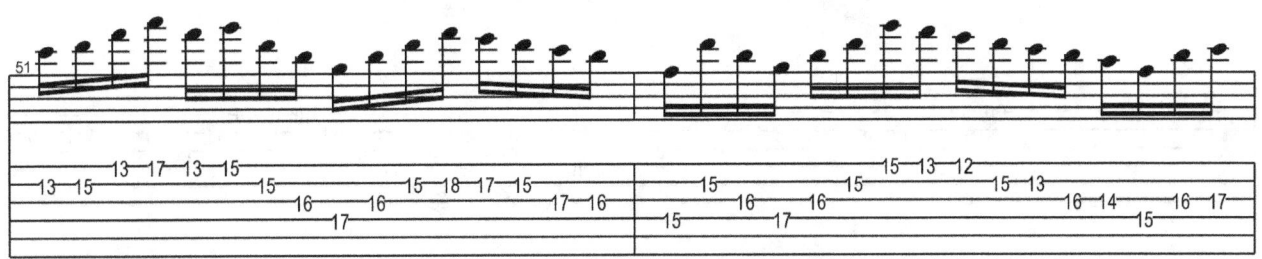
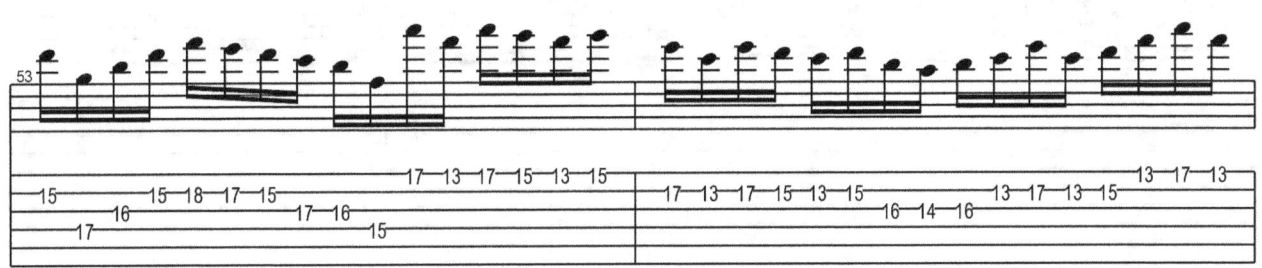
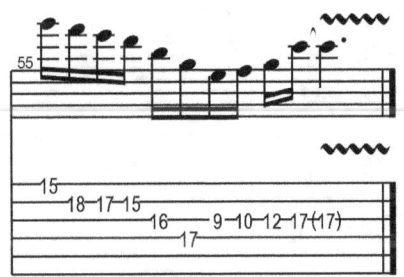

"Caelestis"

Music by Matej Sack

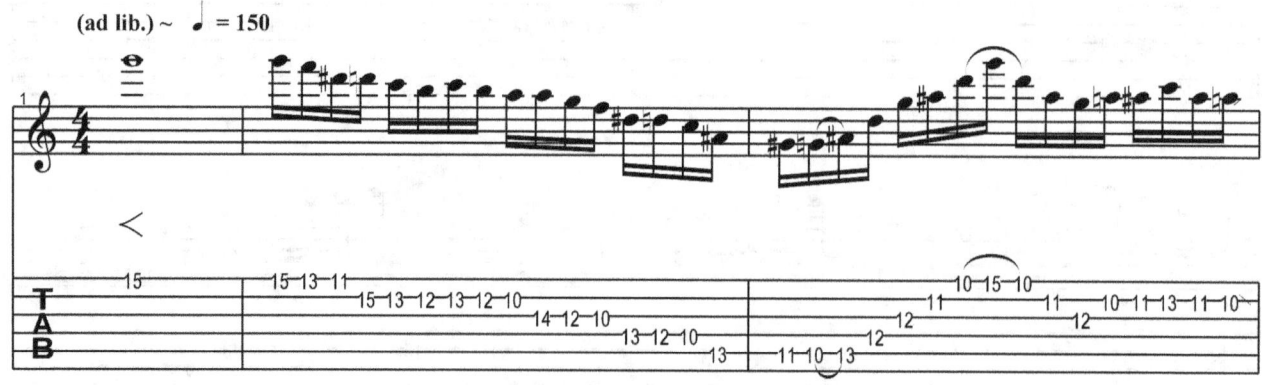
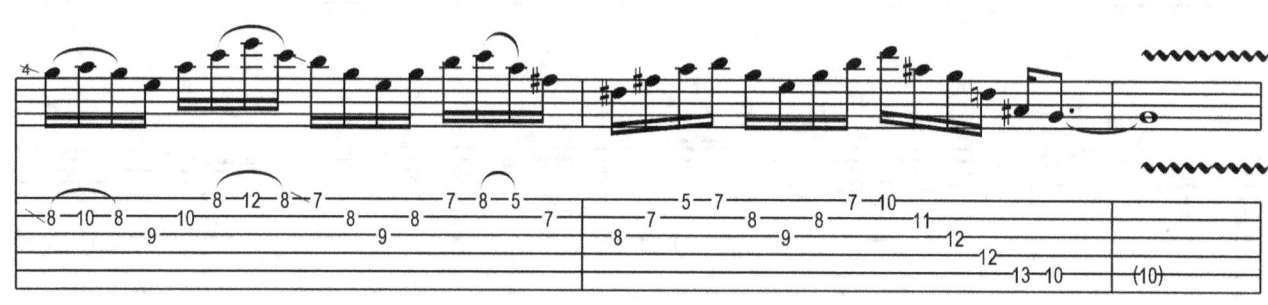
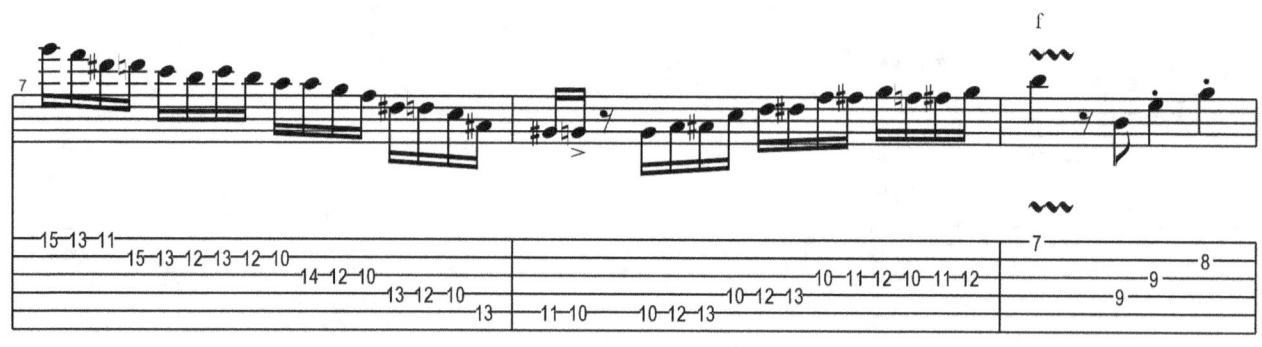
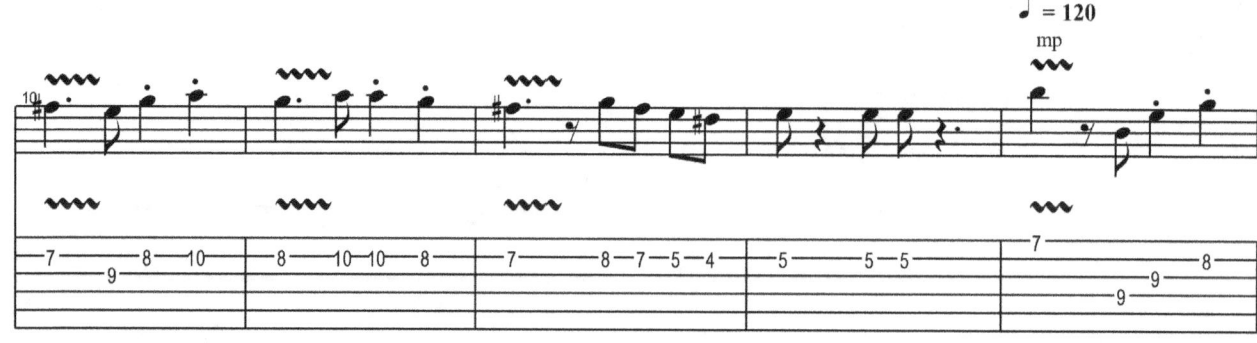

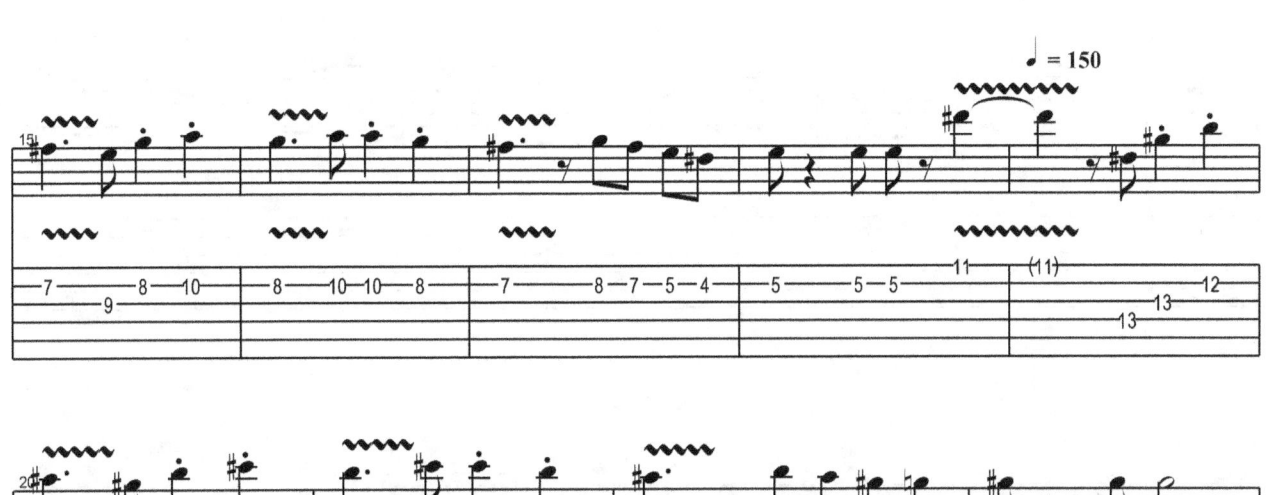
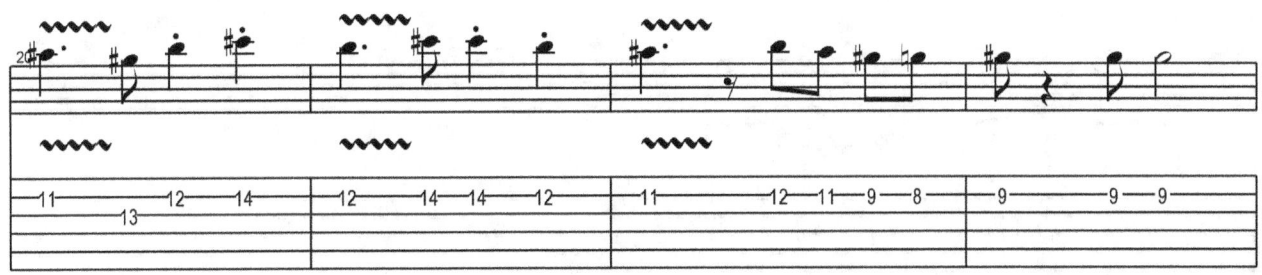
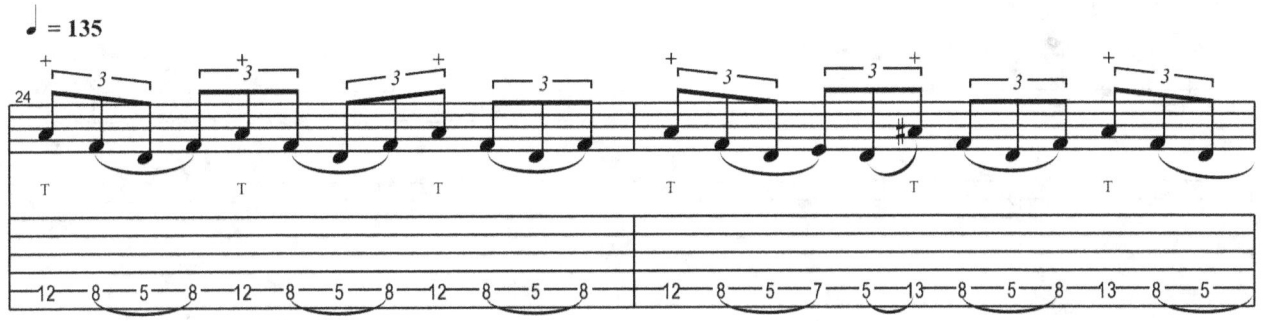
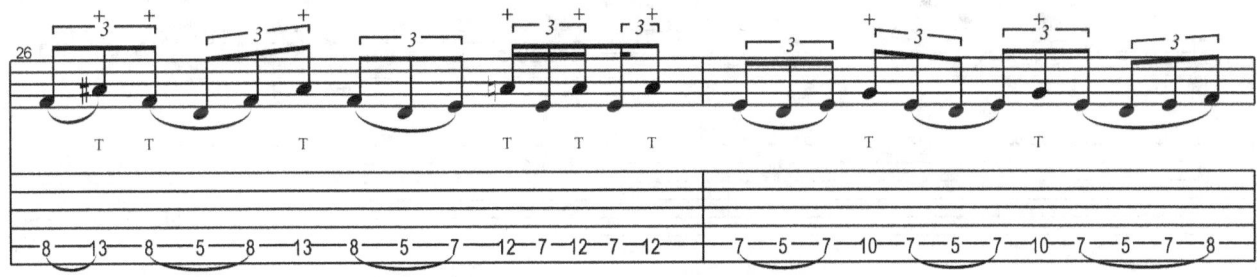
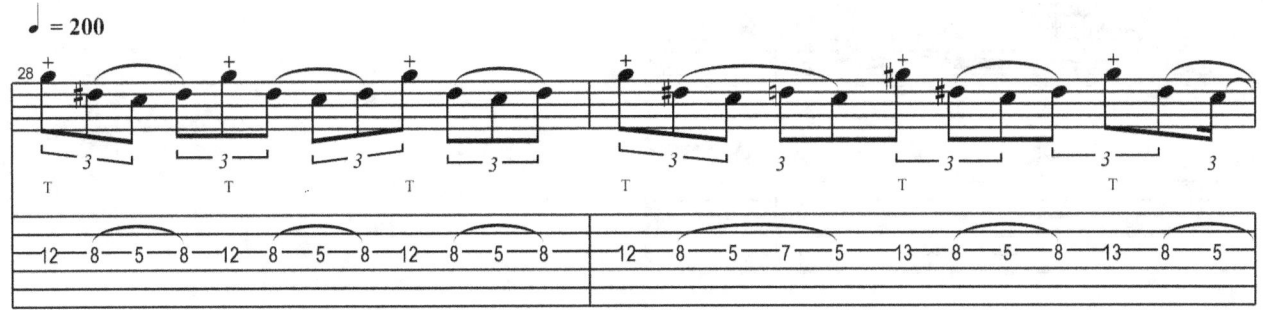

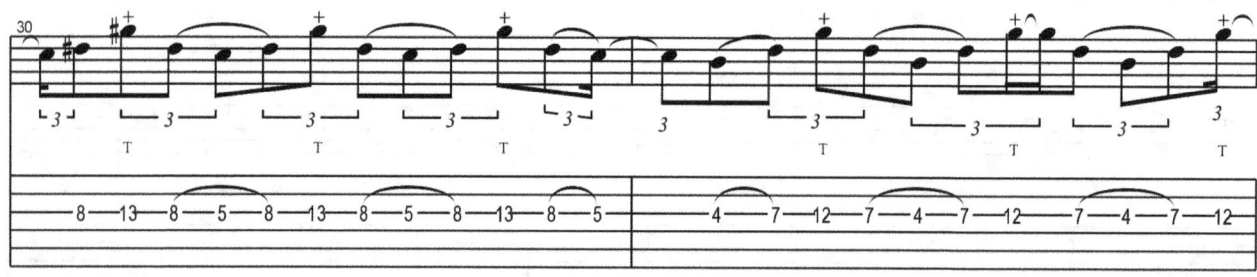
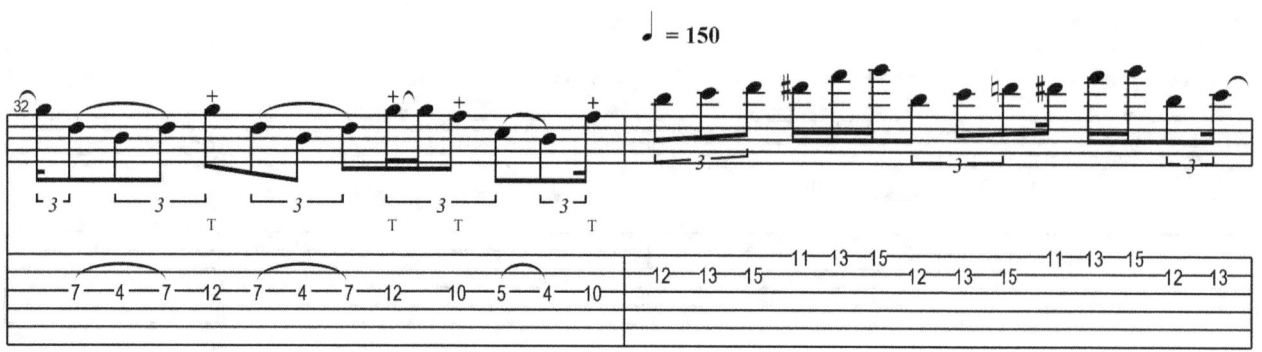
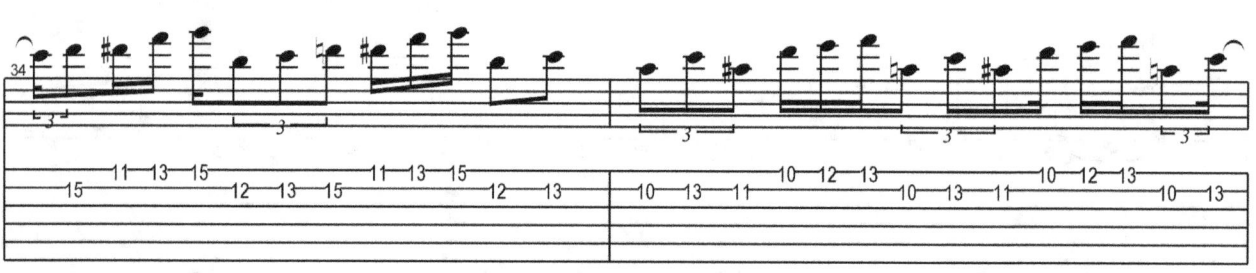
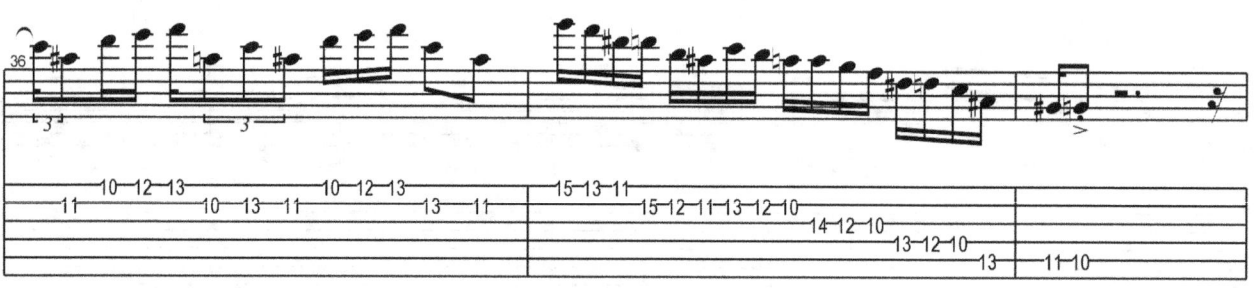
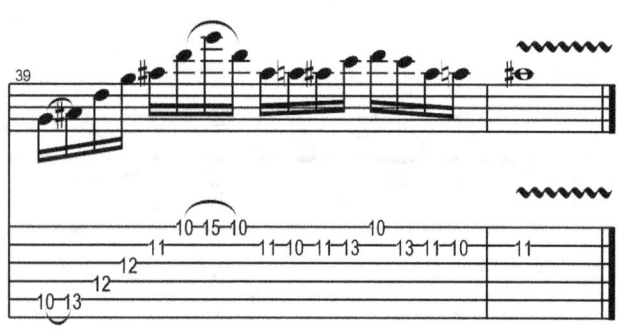

www.ingramcontent.com/pod-product-compliance
Lightning Source LLC
Chambersburg PA
CBHW081816220526
45470CB00007B/2334